P9-EEK-184

KENDO

RECEIVED

JUL 1 2 1999

NORTHWEST RENO LIBRARY
Reno, Nevada

COMPLETE KENDO

by John Donohue

Illustrated by Kathleen Sweeney

Photos by Matthew Donohue

TUTTLE PUBLISHING

BOSTON • RUTLAND, VERMONT • TOKYO

WASHOE COUNTY LIBRARY
RENO, NEVADA

PLEASE NOTE THAT THE AUTHOR AND PUBLISHER OF THIS BOOK ARE NOT RESPONSIBLE IN ANY MANNER WHATSOEVER FOR ANY INJURY THAT MAY RESULT FROM PRACTICING THE TECHNIQUES AND/OR FOLLOWING THE INSTRUCTIONS GIVEN WITHIN. SINCE THE PHYSICAL ACTIVITIES DESCRIBED HEREIN MAY BE TOO STRENUOUS IN NATURE FOR SOME READERS TO ENGAGE IN SAFELY, IT IS ESSENTIAL THAT A PHYSICIAN BE CONSULTED PRIOR TO TRAINING.

First published in 1999 by Tuttle Publishing, an imprint of Periplus Editions (HK) Ltd., with editorial offices at 153 Milk Street, Boston, Massachusetts, 02109.

Copyright ©1999 Charles E. Tuttle Co., Inc.

All rights reserved. No part of this publication may be reproduced or utilized in any form or by any means, electronic or mechanical, including photocopying, recording, or by any information storage and retrieval system, without prior written permission from Tuttle Publishing.

ISBN 0-8048-3148-3
CIP DATA IN PROGRESS

Distributed by:

USA
Tuttle Publishing
Distribution Center
Airport Industrial Park
364 Innovation Drive
North Clarendon, VT 05759-9436
Tel: (802) 773-8930
Tel: (800) 526-2778

JAPAN
Tuttle Shokai Ltd
1-21-13, Seki
Tama-ku, Kawasaki-shi
Kanagawa-ken 214-0022, Japan
Tel: (044) 833-0225
Fax: (044) 822-0413

CANADA
Raincoast Books
8680 Cambie Street
Vancouver, British Columbia V6P 6M9
Tel: (604) 323-7100
Fax: (604) 323-2600

SOUTHEAST ASIA
Berkeley Books Pte Ltd
5 Little Road #08-01
Singapore 536983
Tel: (65) 280-1330
Fax: (65) 280-6290

05 04 03 02 01 00 99   10 9 8 7 6 5 4 3 2 1

Design by Stephanie Doyle
Characters by artist Judith Liniado
Printed in the United States of America

To Kitty, Erin, and Owen:
Masters in the Way of the Heart

CONTENTS

ACKNOWLEDGMENTS

No book is perfect and, with a subject as complex as Kendo, I am sure that this work is no exception. The faults contained here are the product of the author's personal limitations and in no way reflect on the kind assistance I have had from various groups and individuals.

Gratitude is owed to all the people and groups who have assisted (wittingly and otherwise) in this project. First, my thanks go to those (often anonymous) Kendoka who have assisted me in my exploration of this art by their example and their patient teaching. Special acknowledgment is made to Kataoka Noboru Sensei, who serves as a guide for those of us studying Kendo in Western New York today. My thanks go as well to the members of the Buffalo Kendo Club, fellow travelers on this martial path. I am deeply indebted to Kimura Hiroaki Sensei for his warm yet demanding instruction.

Above all, I appreciate the love and support of my wife Kitty and my children Erin and Owen, to whom this book is dedicated.

INTRODUCTION

Kendo (literally the "Way of the Sword") seems to some observers to be the modern martial art that has the most overt links to traditional Japanese culture. Its etiquette, training methods, equipment, and techniques are the product of a long historical development. The philosophical concepts that have helped shape the art and that lie behind its practice are central to Japanese culture. The art of Kendo is not only an exciting and profound discipline on a personal level, it is also an opportunity to gain a great deal of insight into the Japanese character.

What is Kendo? Kendo is the modern, ritualized version of Japanese fencing. There are many Japanese sword arts in existence today. They span the range from true classically-oriented combat systems that attempt to train individuals in traditional Japanese military skills (often termed *bujutsu*) to more modern, specialized systems such as *iaido*, which focuses on the technique and esthetics of drawing the long sword. As a generic term, in fact, Kendo can refer to any system of Japanese swordsmanship. As I use it here, "Kendo" refers to the modern martial art referred to as Nippon Kendo. It can be considered a sport, as well as a physical and mental discipline. It is, in some sense, all of these things. When properly and conscientiously practiced, Kendo is a *Do*, a path or way that can lead the trainee to self-cultivation. It combines the stress and excitement of competition with the potentially profound insights that can be gained from the practice of the Japanese martial arts.

Kendo is not, however, the same art that was practiced by the feudal swordsmen of Japan, the *bushi* or *samurai*. It is a modern system that developed out of these arts, but it is very different. Kendo has rules, combat does not. The restriction of Kendo blows to eight areas has led to a noticeable change in Kendo *bogu* (armor) when compared to the war armor of the samurai. The *shinai*, the bamboo foil used in Kendo, is used differently from a real sword, and is shaped and balanced differently from the *katana*, or long sword of the samurai. Kendo's stance and movements have been conditioned by the fact that *Kendoka* (Kendo practitioners) typically train indoors on a hardwood floor. Feudal warriors fought on battlefields. These are a few examples of technical considerations that have decisively affected the evolution of technique and equipment in Kendo.

All modern *budo* (martial ways) are substantially changed from their feudal predecessors. This does not mean, however, that they are not worth our study or interest. Like any aspect of culture, a martial art such as Kendo is valuable because it is a vivid reminder of the past. It also continues to contribute to human life in the present precisely because of the changes it has undergone in its adaptation to modern conditions. Kendo has its roots in Japan's feudal age, but endures in the modern era precisely because these roots have made it strong enough to bend in the winds of history, and yet to endure. Kendo is linked to the feudal samurai not in substance, but in spirit.

I have consciously attempted to underscore that link by creating a structure for this book that echoes that of Miyamoto Musashi's *Go Rin no Sho* (Book of Five Rings). Musashi's work is widely interpreted in the West today as a book about swordsmanship that is more than just a book about swordsmanship. It has, many feel, applications for strategic thinking and action in numerous disciplines. Musashi himself clearly felt that the insights he gleaned from the events of a violent life had implications for a wide variety of people.

From our perspective today we can argue about the real merits of Musashi's life—one concerned with a seemingly compulsive search for conflict and conquest that left him alone at the end of his life, holed up in a cave, penning notes for unknown generations. We can acknowledge, however, that we can benefit from his experience, even as we question his wisdom. In this sense, I have seen merit in organizing this book into five headings that echo Musashi's chapters—Ground, Water, Fire, Wind, Void.

The reader will note an interpretive tone to this book. This is due to my background. I first became interested in Kendo while conducting research on Japanese culture. I have also trained in a wide variety of Japanese martial arts: *karate-do, judo, aikido,* and *iaido.* My professional studies as an anthropologist (someone who specializes in the description and interpretation of foreign cultures and societies) nicely blended with my personal interest in budo as a vehicle for physical and spiritual cultivation. I found that my studies in Japanese history, language, and culture, combined with the insight generated from the discipline of anthropology, substantially enhanced both my appreciation and understanding of the martial arts.

This advantage was made even more evident when I began to study Kendo. This art is highly formalized, heavily symbolic, and still very strongly linked to traditional Japanese culture. It has been molded by the Japanese historical and intellectual experience.

Very little written material on Kendo is available to nonspecialists outside of Japan, when we compare it to other martial arts. What are available are works of a primarily technical nature, or works on philosophy and the martial arts in general. Comprehensive yet accessible texts dealing with Kendo are rare. One of the many aims of this book is to attempt to partially fill this void concerning Kendo literature in English. In particular, as I put this book together, I kept in mind the questions I had when I began the study of Kendo, the concepts that seemed to help me, and the images that helped me make some sense out of my *dojo* experience. In many ways, then, this is a book that attempts to serve as a basic guide for beginning Kendoka.

I make no claims that this is a definitive work in a technical sense. Kendoka look primarily to their *sensei* for guidance in training. This book is in no way meant to replace the absolutely vital technical and spiritual guidance that the trainee receives in the dojo. At the same time, however, many of my fellow trainees, who were attracted to the art precisely because of its philosophical and cultural depth, lament the absence of any holistic treatment of Kendo.

In the final analysis, I am convinced that the insights I have gleaned as an anthropologist—a grasp of Japanese history, culture, and philosophy, and an understanding of how they relate to the martial arts in general, and to Kendo in particular—could help other martial artists and those interested in Japanese culture come to a deeper appreciation of Kendo.

So this book is "comprehensive" in the sense that I have attempted to provide as complete and balanced a treatment as I could. I do not mean to imply that this will (or should) be the final word on the subject. I do hope, however, that it gives the many people interested in Kendo a clear picture of what the art is and what benefits it provides. If this little book helps in this regard, I shall be very pleased. The Way is long, its significance profound, and I have but begun to walk this path. I would, however, like to share some of the insights I have gained along the journey so far.

地

GROUND

In the *Book of Five Rings*, the famous swordsman Miyamoto Musashi begins his reflections with a consideration of basics. He discusses how the masters of all trades are those who take the time to learn the basic things: a devotion to fundamentals is a hallmark of mastery. They are people intimately familiar with even the tiniest details of their callings. Today, in an age obsessed with speed and immediate gratification, a more measured, careful approach to mastery is sometimes difficult to understand. Nonetheless, the experience of generations of swordsmen bears Musashi's contention out. While we all aspire to mastery, it is appropriate to begin with first things first.

The study of the Way of the Sword opens a number of new worlds to the trainee: new ways of doing things, new customs, new surroundings.

Any worthwhile learning experience is one that is not only challenging and rewarding, but also a bit confusing. Therefore, as the novice Kendoka begins study, a bit of explanation and orientation may be in order.

1 . S W O R D   A N D   S P I R I T

The sword is a living thing. Although a product of man's technical precocity, it is far more than just a tool, a fusion of carbon and metals hammered and shaped into utilitarian form. A sword is a conduit of power. It pulses with the psychic energy of its wielder, and takes on the nuances of that individual. It transforms the holder, investing the swordsman with a form of force that is the result of some occult melding of body and blade. The Japanese tell tales of swords that sing in their scabbards to warn their owners of danger, of blades forged by evil men that do evil deeds, of other swords, created by beneficent smiths, whose razor edges would not cut a leaf innocently borne to them by wind or water. The sword augments our strengths, it magnifies our faults. It is an implement of discipline, a symbol of courage, a tangible representation of justice.

The human fascination with the sword transcends cultural boundaries and time. The magic of Excalibur and the failed quest of Arthur are as compelling now as they ever were. A new generation of children respond viscerally to the power and danger of the Force and light sabers. It is the skill of a master fencer (and true love) that rescues the Princess Bride. Watch the eyes of any child as a sword is drawn from its sheath. What you will see there expresses the power of the sword far more powerfully than any prose: the recognition of beauty, danger, and potential embodied in a gleaming, elementally cruel form.

To attempt to come to grips with the sword in all its implications is to explore peril, fear, and wonder in a fundamental way. The sword is a physical entity whose utilization demands an intense discharge of psychic energy. At the same time that it enhances our power, it also makes us vulnerable to others similarly armed. Because it is a weapon, it confronts us with the terror of mortality and considerations of moral action, often making the linkage between the two painfully real and present.

The sword, as a Yagyu swordsman once said, can both give life and take life. To take up training in the sword, then, is to confront life itself.

2. THE WAY OF THE SWORD

Over centuries, Japanese warriors, or bushi, reflected on and refined the use of weapons. While armed with a variety of fighting tools—the bow, the spear, the halberd known as *naginata*—over time, the professional class of feudal fighters known as samurai developed a special affinity for the sword.

When a samurai boy reached the age of five, he underwent a special ceremony. Standing on a go board, the child was presented with a replica sword, henceforth to be carried as a symbol of his status and his duty.

Of course, for fully adult samurai, the sword was more than a symbol. It was a tangible source of power—the back-country clans of military retainers had literally hacked their way to political primacy in Japan. Their fascination with the weapon had a practical dimension, since it was by skill in military arts such as *kenjutsu* (swordsmanship) that a samurai served his master, provided for his family, and preserved his life (when possible).

Over the years, as a practical need for sword arts faded, the Japanese nonetheless persisted in training. This was because they felt that the pursuit of excellence in technique, the focus needed in matters of life and death, and the discipline required of the trainee had the potential to help the individual transcend questions of protection and lead to a type of spiritual illumination. Even as the feudal era passed away and the Japanese were confronted with the promise and peril inherent in the modern era, they sought to preserve the warrior's training. What evolved were any number of martial disciplines centering on different weapons and many that used the suffix *do* (way) to stress the spiritual element in training.

Budo

Kendo (the Way of the Sword) is the modern martial art that perhaps lies closest to this intent. It is an activity demanding great energy and skill and a fidelity to hard training. Yet it is also a pursuit of spiritual calm in the midst of a duel's heat, of the beauty embedded in flawless technique, and of the humility required in the pursuit of self-perfection. As such, it is emblematic not only of the unique experience of the Japanese, but also of the universal human propensity to create beauty out of the most unexpected materials.

3. EQUIPMENT

Kendoka use the following equipment in their study: a practice uniform, a split bamboo foil for engagement matches, a wooden sword for forms practice, and a four-piece set of armor for protection.

THE UNIFORM

Students of Kendo wear a distinctive uniform that echoes the garb
of the feudal samurai who pioneered the art of the sword. Unlike
the *gi* worn by *karateka* and *judoka*,
the uniform worn by Kendo
trainees consists of the pleated split
skirt known as a *hakama* and a heavy
cotton top referred to as a *keikogi*.
The effect of the long, swirling
hakama is to impart a certain grace
and dignity to Kendoka as they
train. In addition, this piece of
apparel is meant to convey some
inner meaning.

The hakama was part of the formal wear of Japanese warriors. By
wearing it, Kendo students under-

Kendoka in uniform
in jodan no kamae

score the link their training creates between the present and the long tradition of the martial arts in Japan. The hakama has seven pleats in it, and
each pleat is said to stand for one of the Confucian virtues a warrior was
to possess: *jin* or benevolence, *gi* or honor, *rei* or courtesy, *chi* or wisdom,
shin or sincerity, *chu* or loyalty, and *koh* or piety. It is knotted in the front
and, as with many martial arts, this knot is placed near the *hara*, the physical center of balance in the human body as well as the reputed center for
the generation of *ki*, a type of physical/psychic energy.

The hakama is a bit more complex to wear than the pants of a gi. In the first place, there is a right way and wrong way to put one on. You should always put your left leg in first when donning a hakama. When taking it off, you should remove your right leg first. Novice swordsmen who tend to think that this is taking an attention to detail a little too far should know that it is not uncommon during tournaments where students are seeking promotion to have judges observe them dressing in order to check on this aspect of the management of the hakama.

Once you have stepped into the hakama, bring the front panel up to your waist. Bring the strings on either side around to the back. Then pass them around to the front, crisscrossing them, and then back again. They should then be tied behind you. Then raise the back panel, fitting the high, stiff portion of the hakama known as the koshita into the small of your back and above the knot created by the front panel ties. The back ties are shorter. Weave them through the secured front ties on either side of your hips, bring them around to the front, and tie them. There is a variety of knots that can be used in tying the hakama. These different styles of knots convey different meanings regarding a student's affiliation to a dojo or martial art style. In many Kendo dojo however, the knot is simply a square knot. It is formed in much the same way as the knot used to tie the obi, or belt, in karate or judo. As with these belts, the ties on the hakama are knotted in front. The loose ends, however, are tucked in along the sides of the tie tapes.

As a pleated garment, the hakama requires some care. It is not necessary to wash it after every practice. The loose nature of the garment prevents it from becoming too soiled during practice. After a session, hang it up to air. If necessary, the hakama should be washed by hand or on a gentle machine cycle and allowed to drip dry. Hang the hakama up and permit the legs to fall free. To preserve the crease of the pleats, you can clip them together with clothespins as the garment dries.

Folding the hakama for transport to or from practice or tournaments also requires some care to preserve the crisp lines of the uniform. The diagram shows the process of folding the hakama. You can also use special knots to tie it together, also illustrated on the next page.

Hakama folding

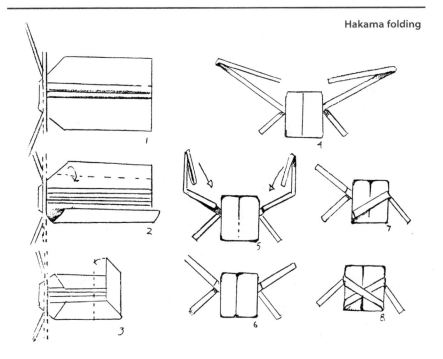

The keikogi is the quilted cotton top worn tucked into the hakama. When one is dressing, the top is donned first, and the hakama is drawn up over it. Keikogi are much like the quilted tops that judoka or *aikidoka* wear, although they have a pair of ties at about chest height on the right side to keep the keikogi neatly in place during practice. The heavy fabric of the top helps in protecting the torso (and particularly the upper arms) from stray blows during matches.

Hakama folding

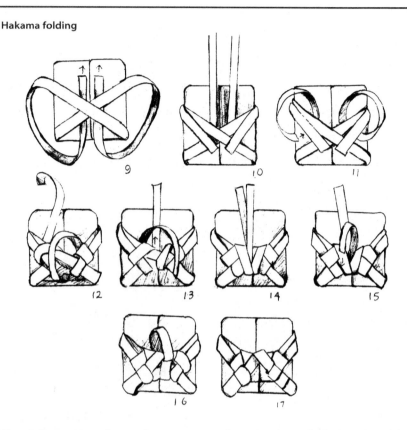

Kendoka wear uniforms that are most often dyed a rich dark indigo blue. The distinctive blue keikogi in Kendo is said to be dyed with a special medicinal pigment known as *aizome*. The dye in the best of these garments tends to rub off on the skin, and is said to help promote healing when a student is bruised or cut during training. Hakama are also dark blue in color, although not dyed with the same substance.

Students, depending on the preferences of their instructors, are also free to wear other colors in training. All black training uniforms, all white uniforms (particularly for women in some dojo), as well as uniforms composed of a hakama of one color and a keikogi of another are also common.

In modern times, children often wear an unbleached white keikogi with black cross-stitching, known as a *shiromusashi*.

The colors worn in Kendo, as in all the martial arts, are types of symbolic statements. The dark blue or black uniform colors are associated with the samurai's traditional role as representatives of social order. Dark blue is also associated with the god Fudo, the immovable. White is thought of as the color of purity and death. Combinations of dark and light are often thought to express the duality of *in-yo* (or *yin* and *yang*), a phenomenon traditionally thought to underlie all existence.

Kendo utilizes the *kyu/dan* system of ranking pioneered in judo and used in many martial arts systems today. Unlike many of these systems, Kendo does not use a system of colored belts to indicate rank. In Kendo, rank levels are demonstrated by performance. Beginners start at sixth kyu and move up in rank through the kyu levels five, four, three, two, and one. At this point, trainees are eligible for dan ranking, the point at which a black belt is awarded in other martial arts. Dan ranks proceed numerically up through tenth dan. At the fourth through sixth dan levels, an individual is entitled to the title *renshi*. At eighth through tenth dan, a Kendoka is given the honorary title of *hanshi*.

Individuals vary in the time it takes to advance in Kendo rank. Generally speaking, it will take from two to three years to advance through the beginner kyu levels. Standards vary from organization to organization, but there is also usually a mandatory time limit that must be spent in training before the next promotion. This is especially true of dan levels, where the amount of time spent in grade gets longer the higher the dan level. It is generally held that kyu examinations below first kyu may be held at individual dojo. For promotion to first kyu and above, however, the aspiring student is required to participate in a promotion *shiai* where Kendoka from a number of schools are tested by high-ranking instructors. This is to ensure that the rigorous technical standards of Kendo are adhered to.

TRAINING WEAPONS

The use of a mock sword known as a shinai is what makes the art of Kendo possible. Japanese warriors traditionally trained with katana (the long sword) and a hardwood replica sword termed a *bokken* or *bokuto*.

Bokken or Bokuto

During the centuries when warriors actively pursued their calling, the process of learning swordsmanship was one that entailed an intense study of basic techniques through solo movements, as well as choreographed patterns with two students, known as kata. Free fighting, while liberated from the constraints of *kata*, was also real fighting. Combatants could use either a real sword or the bokken, but the results were often deadly. Even the wooden training sword can be fatal in the right hands. The famous swordsman Musashi Miyamoto, for instance, used a wooden sword with fatal effect in a number of duels. With live blades, the probability of injury was even higher. Japanese swordsmen figured that, in any duel, they had one chance in three of coming out unhurt. The samurai felt that if two opponents of equal ability crossed swords, the extreme sharpness of the katana probably meant that both would be killed or seriously injured. If a warrior fought someone of superior skill, he expected to die.

Only if the fighter was confronted with an opponent of inferior skill could he hope to emerge unscathed.

Combat, in other words, was the proving ground of sword skill in feudal Japan. Once the country was unified in the seventeenth century, however, the samurai did not have as many opportunities to refine their swordsmanship. Controlled free fighting that was nonlethal was impossible with a real blade, and only marginally better with a wooden one What was needed was a relatively safe training aid that would permit a type of free fighting without fear of injury.

The shinai, a fencing foil of split bamboo bound together with leather, is what emerged. A more detailed description of the evolution of Kendo is presented in Part IV, Wind, but after a century or so of evolution, the shinai was developed in its modern form.

SHINAI SPECIFICATIONS BY CLASS

CLASS	LENGTH	WEIGHT
Adult	<1.18 meters	>468 grams
High School	<1.15 meters	415– 485 grams
Middle School	1.10 meters	300–375 grams

The shinai is different from a real or wooden sword in a number of ways. In the first place, it is longer, the handle having been lengthened to accommodate the protective mitts worn in Kendo. In the second place, the shinai is not really a cutting implement at all. It is roughly tubular, and so has different aerodynamic properties from a real or wooden sword. The shinai is also much lighter than the other two. A glance at the different swords used today in various martial arts concerned with swords-

manship shows an evolutionary progression toward a nonlethal implement that can mimic the action of a sword. What modern Kendoka use,
in other words, is a type of symbolic sword that captures the essence of
the swordsman's intent, but can by no stretch of the imagination be
thought to impart a complete knowledge of swordsmanship. In fact, the
reason for the inclusion of kata training in Kendo is, in part, to familiar-
ize students with how to use a wooden sword, which requires greater use
of the hips and different use of the hands. The advantages of paired work
with bokken, hearkening back to traditional patterns of training, is
emphasized through the study of *kendo no kata* (see Part IV, Wind). Finally,
no swordsman's studies are complete without training in iaido, where real
katana or replica swords known as *iaito* are used.

Shinai and its parts

A. Sakigawa   B. Nakayuki   C. Tsuka

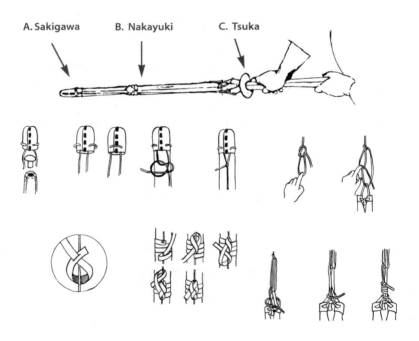

The importance of the shinai (and therefore of Kendo) is that it permits trainees to engage in simulated combat without fear of serious injury. No Kendo sensei would say, however, that this freedom means that the proper attention to proper form and to basic techniques should be overlooked by any serious trainee.

The shinai is made of four bamboo staves bound together. The *saki-gawa* is the covering that is placed over the tip of the weapon. A string runs from the tip down the symbolic "top" of the shinai shaft. About one third of the way down, the staves are bound together by a leather tie known as the *nakayuki*. Finally, the handle, or *tsuka*, also of leather, serves as a place to grip the stave and to hold the base together. The shinai is both a practical and aesthetic object, and there is a specific way of tying the various components together. A basic guide is replicated on page 20.

Trainees should take the time to maintain and care for their shinai. The bamboo staves that are the weapon's main component will splinter after hard use. Before every practice session, the student should carefully examine the shinai and its fittings to make sure that no jagged splinters are exposed. Use a piece of sandpaper or a sharp knife to trim jagged edges. Small cracks that develop in the individual staves can be repaired using carpenter's glue.

The leather ties and string that secure the sakigawa, nakayuki, and tsuka in place should also be routinely checked, tightened, and replaced when necessary. Finally, the shinai should be oiled to keep it from drying out. With proper care (and good technique) a shinai can last the Kendoka for a year or more (although it is always a good idea to have an extra handy, particularly during matches). In recent years, graphite shinai have been produced for serious practitioners. They are flexible and strong, and do not wear like more traditional shinai. They are, however, considerably more expensive than bamboo foils and, because these graphite models are relatively heavy, some Kendoka prefer using bamboo shinai in sparring.

Through the use of the shinai, Kendo students can also replicate the fast-paced, emotionally charged experience of a duel. As anyone who has experienced this sort of competition can tell you, it is a grueling test of an individual's ability to apply the basics of what he or she has learned to a fluid situation.

Ideally, Kendoka should train with all three types of swords. It is particularly important as the student progresses that he or she gain some familiarity with the use of the katana, since handling it effectively is a very different matter from using the shinai. This conviction has led to the well-known saying in Japanese swordsmanship that Kendo and iaido form two wheels of the same cart—both are necessary to go anywhere.

Bogu

BODY ARMOR

Kendo bogu was modeled on the battlefield armor of the feudal samurai. This armor was lightweight and flexible, compared to that worn by European knights, and this tradition has endured to influence modern Kendo's protective coverings.

Bogu today consists of four pieces of equipment: a face and head protector made of metal and fabric that serves as a modified helmet and is called a *men*; a lightweight chest protector called a *do*; a cotton hip protector, or *tare*; and a pair of mitts, or *kote*, to protect the Kendoka's hands and wrists. Clad in the sweeping training uniform of a hakama and keiko-gi and swathed in protective bogu, a kendo trainee cuts an exotic figure that is reminiscent of Japan's feudal tradition (and also seems to have influenced the futuristic costumes of Star Wars).

Bogu represent a significant investment for a trainee—even a set of inexpensive beginner's bogu can run around four hundred dollars—and should be appropriately cared for. As in the rest of the art, there are certain "do"s and "don't"s regarding bogu.

When donning bogu, the student sits in the formal position known as *seiza*. The kote are placed side by side (palms down) in front and to the right. The men is laid face down on the kote. The tare, or hip protector, is put on first. The cords are wrapped around the back, crossed, and brought to the front. They are tied underneath the central flap of the tare.

The chest protector is then put on. There are two cords on each side of the do. The top cord, which is longer, is brought up and across the back and then tied to the loop on the front of the do (the left-side cord tied to the right loop and vice versa). The shorter cords are tied loosely behind the back in a neat bow. When tying the do, the right-hand cord should be tied to the left loop first.

The next step is to put on the men. To absorb sweat and prevent the *himo* (cords) that secure the men from catching the hair on the back of your head, a cotton cloth known as a *hachimaki* or *tenegui* is worn. Tenegui are often given as souvenirs when Kendoka participate in tournaments or visit other dojo.

The student puts on the men, being careful to fit the chin in the rest in the front of the face mask. You should also make sure that the ears lie flat and are not creased inside the men: apart from being uncomfortable, you also run the risk of creating enough pressure to rupture an eardrum if a strike goes astray and hits the side of your head.

The cords attached to the bottom grill of the face mask (the fourth row from the bottom) are brought around each side, wrapped around the back of the head, and then stretched up to the front of the men, where they are put through the top of the iron grid, criss-crossing and leading once again to the back of the head, where they are snugly secured. It is considered good form for the cords not to be twisted and to lie flat. You should also attempt to make sure that the ends of the bow you tie when securing the men are even. A simple way to do this is to pull the loops of the bow out until you can see them in front of you, and make adjustments according-ly. Once the bow is completed, toss the ends back over your shoulders so they hang behind you.

The kote are the last piece of equipment put on. Always put the left mitt on first, then the right. When taking them off, always remove the right mitt first. The pattern here echoes that of stepping into the hakama. It is considered good form to put on your kote this way, since any time you are wearing your right-hand mitt, you are considered ready to spar. Making it the last thing put on signals a definitive readiness to engage in training. In the same manner, by removing the right kote first, when you are ending your activity, you make a clear statement about your intentions. Since the Kendo dojo is, in many ways, a psychically charged environment, clear signals are needed to signify individual readiness.

Removing your bogu in a formal training or contest session is a process we will discuss under Etiquette (see below). When you get your equipment home, however, some special care is needed A vigorous training session wearing bogu tends to make you perspire. When you are finished, you need to permit your armor some time to dry out. The fabric part of the men will often become sweat-soaked. After taking it off, you should lay it face down and let the air get at it, wiping off any surface moisture with your hachi-maki. The palm part of the kote will also be wet. The mitts should be placed face up to dry. Be careful to let your bogu air in a place that avoids direct sun or moisture, since these can damage the pieces.

When storing your dried bogu, there is (as in most things in Kendo) a method.

First the cords of the tare are folded up neatly and secured. The tare is a placed upside down and wrapped across the front of the do. The long do cords are wrapped to the front and crossed over. One cord is drawn up and over the top of the do. The other is drawn under the bottom. These cords are tied in a bow in the center of the do's back. The shorter cords are wrapped around the bottom of the tare and tied in front of the do.

Particularly when the men is new, the side panels (or "wings") for-mally known as *men-buton* need to be bent up when stored so they will fit correctly when worn. The process will be familiar to anyone who has ever broken in a baseball mitt. The kote are placed with the hand por-tion in the bowl created by the face mask. The wings are bent up and forward and tied in place by the strings. The men then fits inside the do for storage.

Bogu, tangible symbols of the heritage of the samurai, should always be treated with care and respect. Especially in the dojo, bogu should be neatly placed in the appropriate manner. Kendoka should be careful never to step over the armor or hit it with their feet, nor should you ever touch anyone else's bogu or shinai without permission.

---

4. THE COMMUNITY OF LEARNERS

KENDO'S DEVELOPMENT

Kendo as a modern martial art, or *shin budo*, is a relatively recent development. Of course, it is widely known that the art has its roots in Japan's feudal past, and some of the dash and exotic flavor of the era of samurai warriors cling to it even today. It evolved from the techniques of swordsmanship developed from the fourteenth through the nineteenth centuries and practiced by a class of professional fighting men. They were known as bushi (warriors) or samurai (a more formal designation of their class).

 Bowing in

We discuss this historical development in the sections of the book entitled Wind and Void.

Briefly, Kendo was developed into its modern form by adopting selected elements of swordsmanship and adapting them to the changing needs of eighteenth- and nineteenth-century Japan. The Abe Ryu was the first to formally designate its system as "Kendo," during the eighteenth century. Prior to this, swordsmanship was generally labeled kenjutsu.

Part of Kendo's development included the adoption of safety features. It was for this reason that fencing gloves and armor were introduced into practice, along with the widespread use of the shinai. The increased margin of safety in practice encouraged training in Kendo even by those who were not professional fighting men, and, by the mid-nineteenth century, a substantial number of Japanese, samurai and commoners, were engaged in what was known as *shinai-geiko*, or the type of training in which students used the shinai and protective armor.

During the nineteenth century, Japan entered the modern world with the collapse of the Tokugawa shogunate and the restoration of the Emperor Meiji. At the same time that the government felt driven to modernize Japan's economy and government, however, there was also a feeling that much that was good in Japanese culture and society needed to be preserved. The particular qualities of courage, loyalty, and discipline that were believed to be encouraged by training in arts such as Kendo were considered vitally important by officials of the Meiji government. As a result, beginning in 1871, traditionalists urged the Japanese Ministry of Education to make Kendo compulsory in all public and private schools in Japan.

Despite this, interest in Japan's martial heritage began to wane in the late nineteenth century, as the Japanese people focused on modernizing their country. Public Kendo exhibitions became common during this period in the hopes of reviving interest, and this may have encouraged a further development of Kendo's evolving "sport" and competition emphasis.

Government sponsorship of these arts eventually served to revive interest. In 1895, the government established the Dai Nippon Butokukai (Greater Japan Martial Virtue Association) in Kyoto, which stressed the role of Kendo and judo in the moral education of Japanese citizens. Making arts such as Kendo and judo part of the education of Japan's young eventually ensured that interest would not die out. In 1905, Tokyo University became the first college in the nation to sponsor a Kendo team, and other colleges soon followed. In 1928, the All Japan Kendo Federation was established as a governing body to regulate and standard-ize the art throughout Japan.

The close involvement of the government with the martial arts caused the Allied Powers to temporarily ban their practice after Japan's defeat in World War II. The aggressive militarism of Imperial Japan during the 1930s and 40s made it seem as if the martial arts had little positive to offer the world, and the attitude of the Allied Powers is understandable. The arts most closely associated with the samurai, particularly those associat-ed with swordsmanship, were proscribed. This ban lasted until 1948.

The fundamentally positive aspect of Japanese budo soon impressed itself upon officials, however, and they came to understand that the excesses of Japanese expansionism could in no way be attributed to budo itself. This process of rehabilitation was aided by the fact that many Allied servicemen stationed in Japan soon became fascinated by the martial arts.

In 1950, the Butokukai was reopened, and judo and Kendo were selected as the primary arts for the training of the newly organized Japanese police force. The rehabilitated image of budo gave rise to increased public participation in these arts. The early 50s saw the first extensive export of budo to the United States. In Japan, the increasing popularity of Kendo and judo was encouraged by a heightened emphasis on sport competitions during the 1960s. The Nippon Budokan, a massive sports arena, was built in 1964 in Tokyo, and is used to host major tournaments in Kendo and judo. As individuals in other countries became familiar with the heritage of the Japanese martial arts, interest in Kendo grew. As a result, the International Kendo Federation was established in 1971. Each nation typically has a ruling body devoted to maintaining the high standards of Kendo and preserving links with the IKF in Japan. Today, Kendo has millions of adherents throughout the world.

As people in the West have been exposed to the Asian martial arts and have come to recognize their value, there has been a steady growth in more "exotic" martial arts forms. In addition, as martial artists who began study in the 1960s and 70s have faced the wear and tear of advancing age, they have begun to look for martial arts forms that do less damage to the body and still offer the physical and psychological benefits of systems such as karate and judo. Finally, large numbers of women are seeking participation in martial arts whose philosophy is attractive and whose techniques enable them to transcend the physical disparities in size and strength between the sexes. All these things have acted to make Kendo increasingly attractive to Western practitioners.

In the United States, the All United States Kendo Federation is the official body regulating the practice of Kendo. It was founded in 1995 when two other Kendo organizations, the Kendo Federation of the United States and the Beikoku Kendo Renmei, were merged. The AUSKF maintains twelve regional Kendo federations, each with a board of directors and officers. Today, there are some two thousand practitioners of Kendo affiliated with the organization in the United States.

THE TRAINING HALL/DOJO

Although Kendo can (and should) be part of everyday life, and can be practiced anywhere, formal training normally occurs in a special location known as a dojo. The name signifies a place for learning a Way (Do), and it should be treated with respect. Every dojo will have its own special details of etiquette (*reigi*), and the process of learning them is a voyage in developing the appropriate respect for the training hall.

Dojo are symbolically divided into zones of higher and lower status. The place of honor in the dojo is variously referred to as the *shomen* or *kamiza*. Its location is usually marked by a small shrine of some sort (hence the term kamiza, which means "deity seat"). Shomen are sometimes designated by a display of some sort, often calligraphy. During ceremonies in the dojo, the sensei sits closest to this special area, and students range themselves in rank order, the lowest ranks being farthest from the shomen. When entering and leaving the practice floor proper, you always bow to the shomen as a sign of respect for the art of Kendo.

Since the dojo is a special place, special behavior is required. Whatever our positions or problems in the outside world, when we enter the dojo, we enter a special realm where all our attention and energies should be devoted in a positive way toward creating an environment where the best is elicited from each of us.

THE DOJO HIERARCHY

As in all Japanese martial arts, there is a pronounced hierarchical emphasis in Kendo. This is demonstrated by the ways in which the class lines up as well as by the ways in which individuals relate to one another in the dojo.

Kendo as an art demands perfection of us, but no one but the most naive of students would believe that the mere practice of this art will lead to perfection. We nonetheless honor Kendo as a way that can help us move further along the path to self-perfection. As a result, we also honor those who have walked this path longer than we have.

In Kendo, seniors are treated with respect. *Sempai* (seniors) are given preference in the day-to-day workings of the dojo. Kohai (juniors) listen to their advice with respect and do their best to emulate them. All trainees treat each other with courtesy and strive to show, even in the littlest things, how Kendo's lessons have influenced their outlook and behavior.

THE GOALS OF TRAINING

Different people look for different things in Kendo training. Some seek the exhilaration of exercise and the challenge of hard physical training. Many Kendo students come to the art after exposure to other types of martial arts. They seek to broaden their knowledge of the martial way and, perhaps, to find a closer link to the samurai experience that they believe created these arts in the first place.

There is room for all these motivations in Kendo. At base, however, it is a special type of martial art. A modern development, it is highly ritualized and codified. It has little immediately practical utility in self-defense. It is an excellent source of aerobic exercise and can present the trainee with an exciting tournament dimension. Most importantly, however, Kendo is a method for disciplining and refining the human spirit. It is this, above all, that it is designed to do.

An excellent summary of the goals of Kendo is provided by the All Japan Kendo Federation:

> *The concept of Kendo is to discipline the human character*
> *through the application of the principles of the katana.*

> *The purpose of practicing Kendo is:*
> *To mold the mind and body,*
> *To cultivate a vigorous spirit,*
> *And through correct and rigid training,*
> *To strive for improvement in the art of Kendo;*
> *To hold in esteem human courtesy and honor,*
> *To associate with others with sincerity,*
> *And to forever pursue the cultivation of oneself.*

> *Thus will one be able to love his country and society, to*
> *contribute to the development of culture, and to promote*
> *peace and prosperity among all peoples.*

Kendo, in short, is not merely about what you can learn to do. It is about what you can learn to be.

水

W A T E R

The symbolism of water permeates writing about the martial arts. Liquid's yielding nature—giving way when pushed—combined with its awesome power seems to embody the adaptive fluidity we seek in martial training. Physically, we need to adapt the characteristics of water. Our minds should emulate the properties of water as well. The proper state for the trainee's mind is *mizu no kokoro,* "mind like water"—that is, calm, unruffled, and perfectly reflecting its surroundings. The message here is that the master martial artist's mind is not roiled with surface distractions. His focus is so perfect that no extraneous and distracting thoughts intrude. Her calm is so perfect that it permits an instantaneous reaction to whatever the opponent does—in much the same way as a calm pool of water immediately reflects whatever is around it. In training, there are a multitude of things that can create the gaps in concentration called *suki*. The way to overcome these gaps is through continuous practice of Kendo's basics, so that our actions and reactions become almost automatic and unthinking—they flow like water.

The process of learning Kendo is at once simple and difficult. It is simple (perhaps "fundamental" would be a better term) because it involves learning how to use our physical and mental capacities in the correct way, and this is something that human beings instinctively respond to and yearn for. Some of my Japanese martial arts instructors said that, no matter how awkward or painful or elusive techniques may initially appear, they are "natural" and so are in reality easy to do. It is only the accretion of bad habits—the result of a life led without training—that makes the acquisition of skill seem difficult. This is, of course, an attitude strongly influenced by both Taoism and Zen.

The process of learning to be natural—of unlearning bad habits—is nonetheless a frustrating and disconcerting experience. It involves the reeducation of the person into different approaches to things as seemingly simple as moving and breathing, balancing and seeing. In some ways, entering into the study of Kendo is like becoming an infant again—we are starting from the beginning and acquiring the skills necessary to be fully human.

THE LESSON

Overview: The basic physical aspect of all Kendo can be understood as being built upon four central elements that form the heart of Kendo's fundamental techniques, or *kihon*:

Stance/Kamae

Footwork/Ashisabaki

Gripping the Shinai/Tenouchi

Swinging the Shinai/Suburi

Beginning students tend to focus on the exterior, flashy aspects of Kendo, but to be effective, these more dynamic manifestations of Kendo's principles must be based on a solid foundation of less glamorous skills.

In the pursuit of Kendo, it is best to go slowly and constantly drill and train in basics: how to stand, how to move, how to wield the shinai. Only a diligent pursuit of these more pedestrian aspects will yield an effective and aesthetically pleasing external form.

Kendo, although simple, in that is based on fundamental principles, is also extremely subtle and complex in the way it brings these principles into action. Since the novice will most often experience this in the process of training, an experience often as confusing as it is enlightening, we will explore the basics of the art by emulating a training session.

I. BEGINNINGS

ENTERING THE DOJO

Most training will take place in dojo of one sort or another. While it is not unusual for practice to be held out of doors in all kinds of weather, the novice swordsman will learn most of his or her early lessons treading the hardwood floors of a traditional training hall.

A dojo is any place set aside for training. The requirements for a Kendo dojo are relatively simple. The ceiling must be high enough to permit the shinai to be swung freely overhead. The floor should be level and smooth. Dojo floors are usually made of polished hardwood. The better ones are loaded on springs to absorb the impact of movement. There is usually an area marked out for sparring matches. Traditional Kendo dojo partake of the structure and simplicity of traditional Japanese architecture. The most significant point in the room is the shomen or kamiza, referred to in Part I, Ground. Movement in and out of the dojo is made in reference to the shomen.

Shomen

The student, garbed in the practice uniform, is ready to embark on the first lesson (see the section on the uniform in Part I, Ground). She begins to step out onto the practice floor.

As in all other aspects of training, there are a number of points to consider here. We will assume that the hakama has been tied properly and that the student is clean and neat and ready to train. Before stepping out, she must first determine where the shomen is located. Movements on and off the training floor are conditioned by this seemingly tangential fact.

There is a right way and a wrong way to enter the training space. The basic underlying principle is that the student should never purposely turn her back on the shomen when entering or exiting. This means that, if the shomen is to your right as you enter, you step in with your left foot (this ensures that your body will be oriented toward the shomen). When you leave via the same route, the shomen will be on your left. Rather than stepping out with your left foot (and thus turning your back toward the shomen) you move your right foot first. If the shomen is located on your left, then the priority of right and left will be reversed. The first rule of entering the dojo properly is to align yourself properly to the deity seat. It is symbolic of the heritage and spirit of the art, and a student's movements need to express a proper respect.

Before stepping onto the floor, bow toward the shomen, inclining your head and back about thirty degrees, hands held at your sides. Many people not brought up in traditional Japanese culture seem to have a difficult time gauging the proper amount of time necessary for a bow. This often creates a type of bobbing effect, in which the trainee does a quick, jerky bow and springs onto the floor. Needless to say, traditionalists find this distasteful and expressive of poor etiquette. I have found that if the novice counts slowly to three while bowing, it creates the image of a proper bow, at least until the trainee begins to grasp something of the spirit of etiquette in budo.

Of course, as you step onto the floor, you are also carrying your shinai. Pure practicality dictates that there must be a way of managing this long object so as to minimize accidents and confusion. In addition, the shinai is considered to be a type of symbolic sword and, therefore, dangerous. Since the student is stepping out onto a floor filled with people similarly armed, it is a good idea to try to communicate something of his intent. Very often in Kendo, you will hear reference to "live" and "dead" postures, or, thought of in another way, as active and passive or aggressive and pacific postures. When you are moving around or on or off the training floor, there are specified ways of holding the shinai that are supposed to be "live" or "dead," as the situation demands. When you are just entering or leaving the floor, you may carry the shinai in a position that shows absolutely no aggressive intent. The shinai is usually wielded with two hands, so a passive grip is normally one-handed. In addition, since the left hand does most of the work of directing the shinai (see below), the right hand is often used to carry the sword when moving around. With your right hand hanging by your side, you grasp the shaft of the shinai in your right hand, the tip pointing down and forward, and the hilt angled up and back. The string that symbolizes the back of a sword is facing to the front, indicating that if this were a real sword the cutting edge would be away from anyone you approached.

When you switch the shinai to your left hand, you signify a readiness for training. The hand is moved up to the hip, the spot where a real sword would rest if it were resting in a scabbard thrust into your belt.

Another passive grip when holding the shinai is known as *hodoku*. It is adopted when training is paused for instructions or corrections from the sensei, or when your training partner indicates a pause for one reason or another. The hodoku posture is also used extensively in Kendo's kata.

This posture is assumed while holding the shinai with both hands. You lower the tip of the sword and point it down and out to the right, at about the level of your knee. The significance here is that this is an extremely awkward posture to try to attack someone from, and it therefore indicates that you are not on the offensive.

Kendo is considered to be an art practiced by refined individuals. This sense of elegance and refinement is emphasized in the precision of technique demonstrated by advanced trainees. It is accentuated through the traditional uniform, which lends a certain grace and swirl to the movement of students. Above all, it is reinforced by the deportment of Kendoka, whether in everyday training or in contest. As part of this emphasis on elegance, warmups in Kendo are not as extensive as those performed in other martial arts.

In fact, warmup exercises, while done, are conducted before the formal beginning of training. Even then, they are cursory in nature, and emphasize the loosening up of the arms and shoulders, the stretching of the back and legs, etc. They are performed with the trainees forming an inward-facing circle. All stretches are performed in a standing or squatting posture—there is none of the intense seated stretching you may have witnessed in karate or judo classes.

During warmups, you also practice swinging the shinai correctly, bringing it up and behind you until it strikes your back, and then forward down to the floor. The sensei may also have you practice a series of strikes to the head (*shomen-uchi*) and alternate strikes to either side of the head (*sayu-men*). Finally, students often perform an exercise known as *haya suburi*, during which you are expected to leap in to strike at the head and then out again, maintaining proper stance and technique, in rapid repetition.

B O W   I N

Following this, the class is called to order by the highest-ranking student present. As in most modern martial arts, pupils line up in rank order facing their instructor, who sits before the shomen. Students line up carefully, and sit in the formal seiza posture when the command is given. In Kendo, whenever you sit or stand, you do it in such a way that you would always be able to draw a sword if attacked unexpectedly. Since the sword was traditionally worn at the left side (and this is where the shinai is held), you kneel down by bending the left leg first—with one leg down, you would still be able to draw the sword freely with your right hand. When you are getting up, the right leg is raised first for the same reasons. When seated, the students make sure that they are in a straight line (gauging their position in reference to their seniors), placing their shinai with the tip pointing behind them and the hilt lined up with the knee.

At the command *moku-so*, students bring their open hands together in their laps facing up, left hand on bottom, thumbs touching, and close their eyes for silent meditation. The shout *yame* (finish) calls them to attention. At the command *rei*, the trainees perform the seated bow, being careful not to expose the napes of their necks to the instructor. At the same time, the class says *onegaishimasu* meaning "please practice with me." The lesson begins.

2. BASICS/KIHON

STANCE/KAMAE

The way in which we stand indicates something of our relationship with ourselves, others, and the world. Stance, the basic physical posture in which we face life's challenges, is an extremely important part of Kendo training. Through this art, we attempt to develop a stance that reflects our mental and spiritual aspirations, that is, we strive for a stance that is balanced, flexible, and allows us to respond effectively to any and all challenges.

One of the most fundamental skills to master in Kendo is the stance. While a beginner's attention is often focused on the flashier elements of the art and fixated on the motion of the shinai in a skilled swordsman's hands, it is, in reality, a stable stance that permits the effective delivery of a strike. There is, in fact, an old Kendo maxim that maintains "in order to learn the techniques, execute your footwork first rather than your handwork." Stance is the foundation of the critical development of footwork.

There are five basic stances in Kendo. *Chudan no kamae* (or *chudan*, the middle stance) is the most commonly used and the one we will focus on here. *Jodan no kamae* (or *jodan*, high stance), *gedan no kamae* (*gedan*, low stance), *hasso no kamae* (*hasso*), and *wakigamae* are more advanced stances that will be discussed in Part IV, Wind. All stances are taken with the sword in hand, but for the moment we will discuss only the position of the body without a discussion of the shinai.

In chudan, the Kendoka stands with the right foot advanced slightly in front of him. The foot is flat on the floor, although the weight is shifted slightly forward so that the heel is barely in contact with the ground. The feet are approximately a hips' width apart. The left foot is placed about twelve inches behind the right toes, and the heel of this foot is raised up about an inch and a half, giving the Kendoka a feeling of being poised for a frontal attack.

Chudan no kamae

The torso is kept upright, the head is level, and the knees are slightly bent to create a feeling of springiness and flexibility in the stance.

Jodan no kamae

Gedan no kamae

Hasso no kamae

Wakigamae

Students of other martial arts such as karate will note that the Kendo stance is relatively shallow and does not "brace" the body, as is done, for instance, in the front stance of various karate styles. The fact that the feet are parallel and are not usually placed in the *hanmi* position also makes it different from the stances commonly used in aikido.

Basic stance—feet (front)

Basic stance—feet (side)

FOOTWORK/ASHISABAKI

Novices will notice that senior Kendoka shoot rapidly across the dojo floor in a type of shuffling glide. The characteristic Kendo style of movement is known as *okuriashi*. Judo practitioners will be familiar with a similar type of shuffle step from their training. In this method of movement, the feet always maintain their position relative to one another. For example, if your right foot is leading, rather than stride forward with your left (bringing that up to and through the center of balance so that it is now in front), you instead slide your right foot forward and then bring your left foot forward the same distance as you moved the right, so that your feet remain in the same position relative to one another. Okuriashi (what we will term a "step" in this book) is different from *ayumiashi* (which we will term a "stride")—the way we typically walk.

Basic Footwork

Kendo uses this gliding step as a means of keeping the swordsman constantly balanced and ready for attack. It is a formalized technique made possible by the fact that the art is typically practiced on smooth hardwood floors in a dojo and not over rough terrain, where a wider stance and a different method of movement would be needed. The rough and ready may object that okuriashi is a type of abstraction, but here is one of the points where the "art" dimension of Kendo enters training. To master this type of movement is a challenge, but it is one that eventually will create both efficient technique and a type of beauty in movement.

To practice the stepping motion of Kendo, keep the knees soft and supple. Weight is almost evenly distributed, although there is a shade of emphasis on the front foot, giving the student the feeling that she is about to explode forward in a strong attack. From the basic position, slide the right foot forward about twelve inches, keeping the knee bent. Maintain contact with the floor using the ball of your foot. Keep the torso straight and the head erect. As the foot is planted, quickly slide the rear foot up, being careful to keep the heel elevated, and end in a position exactly like the one you started from.

In the beginning, before you have developed the calluses on your feet that come with practice, you may have difficulty sliding along the floor. Your feet may stick. Heat and humidity, may also cause this to happen. In this situation, novices appear to gallop across the floor, bouncing up and down. The challenge here is to adjust your balance and make your knees supple. Very often your feet will stick because you are not properly balanced and have placed too much weight on one foot or the other. Remember to glide and maintain the proper weight distribution. With practice (and some good calluses) you will learn to emulate the gliding step of your seniors.

In all the martial arts, movement comes from the hips, and Kendo is no exception. Particularly in the beginning, when you are concentrating on the theory of movement, you will tend to bounce up as you move, almost as if the very power of your thinking pulls you up. Remember to try to keep your hips level and your knees slightly bent. Your legs perform an action like an inverted scissors in this movement. Your right foot moves forward, opening the scissors. Then your left foot slides forward, closing the scissors again. What you must do is remember not to let this scissoring action make you bob up and down. The purpose of the action is to move *forward* in as straight and level a manner as possible—not up, down, and forward, since this will make your technique slow and inefficient.

Lateral movements are made in essentially the same essential manner, maintaining the okuriashi style of movement. Kendoka may sometimes stride forward (ayumiashi) to close the distance between themselves and an opponent, but once within range they will revert to the stepping motion we have discussed here.

In basic practice, trainees will first practice moving forward and backward so that they may accustom themselves to the Kendo way of movement. After this, they will practice moving forward in rapid consecutive steps and then back in the same way. It is not unusual to see a line of Kendoka sliding forward and then back across the whole length of a dojo, practicing this very important basic technique of movement.

GRIPPING THE SHINAI/STATIC SUBURI

Of course, the whole purpose of this movement is to enable you to bring your shinai or bokken to bear on an opponent. In the martial arts, stance and movement are ways of creating a platform and delivery system for the use of a particular weapon. In Kendo, that weapon is the sword (or its various permutations). We will now discuss the ways in which these weapons are wielded.

Let's focus on the shinai. The bamboo mock sword used in matches in Kendo is a cylindrical weapon of split bamboo, held together with leather. In modern Kendo, the length and weight of shinai are carefully regulated (see the chart in Part I, Ground). Length and weight vary with the size and age of the trainee. All students will notice, however, that the handle, or tsuka, is quite long. This is to permit room for both hands when wearing the protective mitts, or kote.

To grasp the shinai, stand in the correct posture. Hold the shinai by the end of the tsuka with your left hand, and place the tip (kissaki) on the floor in front of you. Your left arm should be comfortably extended to the front and center of your body, and the shinai should slant forward. Grip the shinai as you would a baseball bat, fingers pointing down, and grip the handle with the web of your hand, squeezing the shaft between the base of your thumb and your hand. Close your fingers around the handle, gripping snugly with your last two fingers (which should be right at the end of the tsuka) and keeping your middle and index fingers, as well as your thumb, relaxed yet firm.

Gripping the shinai

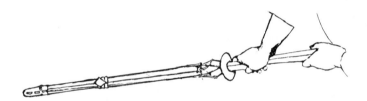

Bring your right hand up over your head and then down in front of you. Place it above the left hand on the tsuka with a gap of about a hand's width between them. Grip the handle in the same manner. Your right hand should be almost up to the hilt (*tsuba*). A good way to check placement is to hold the shinai up in your right hand and place the butt of the handle in the crook of your arm. This will show you about how far up the handle you should place your right hand.

Once you have got the hang of gripping the shinai, raise it up, keeping your hands centered on the body, and point the tip of the weapon at the throat of an imaginary opponent. Your arms should be relaxed and slightly bent, and your left hand should be about a fist's distance away from your navel. The base of each thumb is placed along the top part of

Gripping the shinai

the handle so that your wrists are not bent. The torso is erect, the hips have a feeling of being slightly thrust forward, the shoulders are square with the hips, the chin is level, and the gaze is direct. This is chudan.

You are now ready to swing the shinai in the practice stroke. This is known as *suburi*.

From chudan, raise the shinai up above your head. The fists should come up to a point slightly forward of and above your head, with a space of about a fist between your hands and your head. Your hands shouldn't get in the way of your vision. It is important to swing the shinai up and back this way to maintain proper form, and also because if you do not get into the habit, you will not clear the *men* (helmet) when you are wearing your Kendo armor.

When you swing the shinai up, it should point back and up at about a forty-five degree angle. In warmups, we swing the shinai all the way back, sometimes so far that it slaps the back, but this is to stretch the back muscles. Swinging the shinai too far back when actually practicing represents a waste of motion and effort, since it will mean that the weapon has to travel much farther as it comes forward to deliver a stroke.

When the shinai has been brought up properly, bring the hands down again, swinging the shinai in an arc that stops at the top of the head of an imaginary opponent. Shout "men!" This is the first basic strike to the top of the head, the men strike.

When striking in Kendo, you should have a light yet firm feeling. The wrists, which tend to roll outward when you swing the shinai up, come back in as you strike forward and down, almost as if you were wringing a towel. It is important not to "break" the wrists by bending them too much. At the moment of the strike, they are firmly set in the same position they assumed in chudan: fingers pointing down, gripping the handle with the web of your hand, squeezing the shaft between the base of your thumb and your hand, fingers closed around the handle, gripping snugly with your last two fingers with the other fingers relaxed, yet firm. Your arms are extended, elbows slightly bent, and your fists are in front of you at about shoulder height.

The hardest point for the novice (particularly the right-handed novice) to grasp in this exercise is the fact that the left hand does most of the work in striking. There is a very common tendency to try to muscle the shinai *down* in an arc with the right hand. Yet, in Kendo, the factors that make a stroke effective are not muscular strength, but coordination and speed. In striking, the hands gripping the shinai are raised up and down along the center line of the body in a relaxed manner. Tension and the overuse of muscles only slow the motion down and tire out the arms. When practicing basic strokes, therefore, the beginner should concentrate on keeping the arms (particularly the right arm) relaxed and swinging in an easy motion. The tip of the shinai should describe a straight line as it rises and falls. If you practice in front of a mirror, this will aid you in developing proper technique. Very often too much tension in one hand or another is revealed in the fact that the shinai wanders from one side to the other as you try to strike. Think of your left hand pulling on the rope that rings a bell: it merely travels up and down in front of you. Your right hand simply guides the shinai in its arc forward; it exerts no pressure.

In fact, although we are bringing the tip of the shinai down, the feeling of a men strike is analogous to that of casting a fishing rod. The left hand rises and falls down the center line of the body; the right hand "throws" the shinai out and forward. It feels as if we are propelling the shinai forward at about shoulder height. And, in truth, we are extending our arms to close the distance between ourselves and the target point on our opponent.

When this basic technique has been learned, it should be practiced on a daily basis. Literally thousands of strokes (if not millions) go into the development of good technique. Once you are comfortable with swinging the shinai from a standing position, the time has come to integrate this motion with forward and backward movement. Doing suburi standing still is like a snapshot of technique at the moment a strike occurs. In reality, of course, you and your opponent are moving. It is now necessary to practice a more dynamic form of suburi, taking Kendo practice from the realm of still life into that of motion.

DYNAMIC SUBURI

In uniting the motion of striking with the shinai with that of the Kendo step, the novice faces a significant challenge of integrating what have up to this point been a series of isolated actions. Now, by uniting the actions of the arms and legs, the trainee begins to approximate the actual motions that will be used in a Kendo match.

Starting in chudan no kamae, the Kendoka slides the right foot forward. At the same time, the shinai is raised overhead. As the rear foot is drawn forward in the okuriashi method, the arms are brought down, so that the strike (in this case to men) is completed at the same time that the step is finished. There is a type of squeezing sensation to this motion, of opening the stance as you step forward and raising the arms, and then bringing everything together with the simultaneous completion of the step and the strike.

Be careful not to let yourself rise up as the shinai is raised: keep your knees bent and your hips low. Move forward, not up and forward. Keep in mind the proper way to grip the shinai. Make sure that you end the strike properly. At the completion of the technique, bring the shinai back into the chudan position.

The basic nature of dynamic suburi is an easy one to grasp. By executing multiple and rapid suburi, you will learn the timing and coordination necessary for good Kendo. Execute moving suburi the length of your practice space. Try to execute the motions smoothly and make sure that the cut is completed as the left foot slides into place at the end of the motion. At the beginning you will find that this is difficult to do, especially as your concentration falters after numerous repetitions. Remember the scissors analogy: as the shinai comes up, the scissors open; as it comes down, they close.

Moving backward and executing suburi is a similar challenge. Here the rear (left) foot slides back at the same time that the shinai is raised. As the right foot moves backwards, the shinai is swung down, completing the strike as the foot movements come to an end.

STRIKING POINTS

Once the novice has grasped the basic points of this exercise, she is ready to alter the spot of attack to reflect the target points used in Kendo. By striking these areas accurately, with proper technique and appropriate focus, the Kendoka scores points in contest matches.

Kendo is a formalized system, and it places limitations on which areas of the body can be struck. Since Kendo is designed to present practitioners with little physical risk, and since its philosophy of creating refined individuals requires it, Kendoka only strike in a few sanctioned areas where the bogu of modern Kendo affords the wearer adequate protection.

Striking points

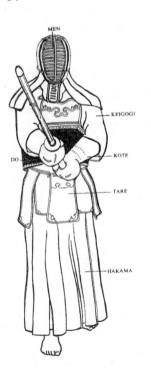

When striking with the shinai, a blow is considered effective only when you strike with the upper third of the shinai—the section from the knot known as the *nakayuki*, extending up past the leather cap of the shinai, the *sakigawa*, to the point.

The head or men target may be struck in three places: the top center or on either side of the top of the head. We have discussed the men strike proper. To strike the right or left side of the men (*migi* or *hidari* men) we use a technique known as *sayu-men*. Here, the shinai is brought straight up over the head as in a men strike, then brought down at a slight angle (think about cutting the head at a forty-five degree angle that would enter at about the eyebrow). Practice alternating strikes to the left and right men, being careful to keep your left hand centered as you extend for the strike. Make sure you extend your right arm as you strike, since there is a strong tendency in doing this exercise to keep the arm bent as an aid in pulling the shinai back to prepare for the next strike. When bringing the shinai back up, follow the same straight line—don't whirl it back and around in a circular motion. The idea here is to keep your intentions hidden. By always bringing the shinai back the same way, you don't give the opponent any advance notice of what you intend to do.

Sayu-men

The right wrist or kote may also be struck. You may hit the left kote, but only when it has been raised (usually above the shoulder). Technique for the kote strike is similar to that for the men: raise the shinai up and down in as straight a line as possible. Strike the wrist portion of your opponent's kote while shouting out your target: "kote!"

Men

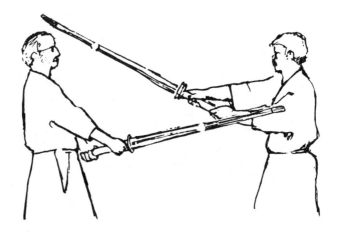

Kote

Do

Tsuki

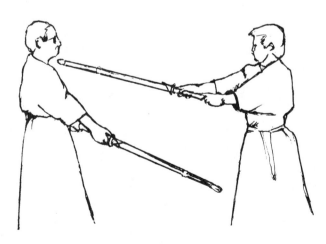

The do, or chest protector, may be struck on the right side. While it is possible to strike the left do, it may only be done in special circumstances and, in all practicality, is a difficult point to make in shiai (contest). In the do strike, there is strong temptation to attempt the strike by hitting sideways. This is an error. The do strike should come down from the same high position as a men or kote strike. The shinai describes a shallow angle that almost grazes the opponent's elbow. The wrists are rotated slightly so that the striking edge of the shinai (not its side) strikes the chest protector. As the stroke is executed, cry "do!"

Finally, a lunge to the throat (*tsuki*) is permitted. The tsuki point is a difficult one to make accurately and cleanly. In the execution of this technique the hips drive the point of the shinai into the protective flap on the front of the opponent's men. Shout "tsuki!" (It sounds like "tski"). Upon contact, the shinai is withdrawn sharply, arms bent in chudan. A crisply executed tsuki is a powerful technique. Kendoka should be careful to practice accuracy in their movements, since it is possible to injure your partner with an inaccurate tsuki. In addition, since this technique will tend to rock the opponent's head back if he or she is not braced for the strike, caution should be exerted when practicing with smaller or younger Kendoka. It is, in fact, advisable not to attempt tsuki against novice, young, or small Kendoka.

SPIRIT

In Kendo, we demonstrate focus and commitment by using a particular shout. Students who have trained in other martial arts will be familiar with the *kiai* used when delivering a technique. In Kendo, we shout to demonstrate spirit at any given point in a match, but particularly when we face off against an opponent and when we launch an attack. Particularly during an attack, it is customary to cry out the target area being assaulted as the strike goes home. This demonstrates a consciousness of purpose and precision that is highly valued in Kendo. This shout is formally known as the *kake-goe*.

One of my most memorable experiences when first being introduced to the art of Kendo was watching a line of somber, graceful trainees erupt into an explosion of fierce cries as they began sparring. Strong spirit in Kendo is made manifest, not only through effective technique, but by the vigor of the shouts of Kendoka.

3 . TECHNIQUES / WAZA

STRIKING PRACTICE

After a beginner starts to grasp the fundamentals, she will have the opportunity to practice actually striking targets from both a static and a moving position. It is only by striking against something, in fact, that we can see how good our technique is.

Some dojo have striking dummies for basic practice of this type. Others pair up students and have one Kendoka hold out a shinai to be struck by the other. This exercise often begins in a still position. Trainees practice men strikes, sayu-men, etc. Then they begin moving forward and backward while executing the same techniques.

The focus here is on learning how to correctly wield the shinai and how to set the hands so that the blow is a focused one. Some basic items should be of primary concern: you need to be careful to use the left arm more than the right in your strikes; you must make sure that you hold the shinai properly and do not break the set of your wrists; you must ensure that the shinai strikes its target and does not bounce off; and you need to make sure that the strokes are delivered with the proper timing as you step forward and back.

The focus of your strokes is important and reveals the extent to which you have grasped the fundamentals of Kendo. If you try to muscle the shinai down to its target, you will hit it far too hard, tiring your muscles and putting excess wear and tear on your weapon. Your technique will also be slow and inaccurate. As your left hand pulls the shinai down, you must extend your right arm so that it feels as if you are pushing the shinai toward the target. Set your hands so the shinai does not bounce off what it strikes.

Paired practice also has the virtue of teaching us something about distance, a critical element in Kendo. When preparing to work with another, you should assume chudan. Your shinai should cross your opponent's just below the sakigawa. At this distance, you can strike your opponent by taking one step in toward her.

Working with a partner means that you will be receiving strokes as well as giving them. Use this opportunity to work on your footwork and posture. Also note the timing of your partner as he moves in to deliver a stroke. Finally, you can help your partner by observing her technique and helping to make it better, since you may be able to spot something that she cannot.

---

4 . PRACTICE / KEIKO

UCHIKOMI

The next step is to practice your technique in bogu. If a beginner does not yet wear bogu, his seniors will nonetheless permit him to strike them when they are wearing armor. This permits the trainee to become comfortable with striking the correct points. This formal type of attack practice, or *uchikomi*, is a useful way to polish technique.

Kendoka typically start practice wearing the do and tare. The men and kote are placed along the wall of the dojo in such a manner as not to interfere with the training. The kote are placed side by side with the palms down. The men is placed, grill down, on top of the kote. The cords of the men should be neatly placed inside it, and the hachimaki or tenegui is either folded up inside the men or opened up and draped over it.

At the command to don armor, students retrieve their men and kote. They kneel in the seiza position, placing the shinai to their left. The men and kote are placed in front and to the right of the Kendoka. Put on the tenegui, being careful to fold the ends in, so they will not stick out of the back of the men. Put on your men, then your kote (left one first), pick up your shinai, stand, and await a partner.

It is somewhat difficult to hear wearing bogu, so hand gestures are often used to communicate. It is important to know that, if something is wrong with your bogu—a string comes untied, your men is not fitted properly—or with your shinai—it is cracked or any of the leather or string fittings break—you signal a halt to proceedings by taking your right hand from the shinai and holding it up by your right shoulder. If you need to adjust your bogu, sit down in the seiza position and do so. When it is secure, stand up, hold your shinai in hodoku, and bow to signal your readiness to continue.

In practicing uchikomi, each partner should strive to give the other a chance to score a clean hit on the proper target. Depending on the level of accomplishment of the Kendoka, this usually means presenting an opening for the strike to occur. For a men strike, the receiver will lower the shinai slightly to permit the attacker to score. For kote, the shinai is often raised up and tilted slightly to the receiver's left to offer the opening. For do practice, the receiver usually raises the shinai into the jodan position.

As you practice, listen to the sound your stroke makes. A properly placed stroke will make a popping sound on the top of the men or on the kote. A good do strike will also make a clear sound. Make sure that you are using good technique. Pay attention to your timing and distance, and take care that you are hitting with the correct part of the shinai.

As you practice uchikomi, an important part of technique that needs to be developed is the follow through. The spirit of Kendo is that of total commitment. So when you strike your partner, there can be nothing tentative about it. The way we exhibit this commitment and this focus is through the practice of *zanshin*. In Kendo, zanshin is demonstrated through the quality of the follow-through in a technique.

When striking men, you should continue to advance with the feeling that you are going through your opponent. That is, immediately after stepping forward and striking, you continue to step in okuriashi fashion at least several steps beyond the opponent, hands held high and focused on the correct position for a men strike. You then wheel around to face him with the shinai at chudan.

When you turn, you always turn towards the opponent. So if you pass your partner on your right, you will turn toward your right when you wheel around. If you do so on the left, you will wheel toward the left.

When striking kote, after the hit you pull the shinai up and to your left slightly, pass your opponent to your left, continue through and wheel around.

After giving a do stroke, you may pass on either side. If you pass to your left, the zanshin position for the shinai is the same as for kote. If you are passing to your right (diagonally across your opponent's front), your right hand crosses over your left so the shinai maintains contact with the opponent. As you move past, the tip of the shinai faces to your rear. You maintain this orientation of the weapon and then turn to your left so that you finish the technique by turning to face the same direction the shinai does.

We practice formally from a distance at which one step will bring you to within striking range of your partner. In a contest, however, this will not always be the case. To close the distance, it is sometimes necessary for you to take a lunging step forward, landing with a stamp of your leading foot. It is important when executing this advance to spring forward (not upward), to maintain a proper stance, and to lead with your hips. In a lunging movement of this type, the temptation is very strong to lean in toward the strike, but this should be avoided. Also be careful to land flat on your leading foot to avoid bruising your heel, especially on floors or other surfaces that do not float or yield.

KIRIKAESHI

A formal type of paired practice observed wherever Kendoka train is known as *kirikaeshi*. Traditionally, it was said that three years training in kirikaeshi was necessary for a student to gain a good grasp of Kendo's fundamentals. Whether one is attacker or receiver, kirikaeshi is thought to provide Kendoka with a number of benefits. In the first place, it reinforces habits that lead to proper technique. It gives both participants experience in judging timing and distance. It provides an opportunity to display spirit and zanshin. Since it is fast-paced, kirikaeshi also helps the Kendoka develop stamina.

Basically, kirikaeshi is a very simple exercise. Two Kendoka pair off, engage in a series of movements, and then reverse roles.

The pair assume chudan, shinai crossed. The attacker shouts "men!" strikes that target, and advances into the opponent, hands extended in good zanshin about chest height, pushing the receiver back. The two adjust their distance, and the attacker steps forward four times, attacking men each time. The blows alternate: first the attacker strikes to his right to hit the receiver's hidari-men, then to his left to hit the opposite side. After four strikes, the attacker steps backwards five times, striking men with each step. After the fifth stroke, the two adjust their position, and the attacker steps forward to attack with another men. Then the entire sequence is repeated.

After the second repetition, the attacker launches a final men attack. This time, the attacker goes "through" the receiver, passing back on the receiver's left side, exhibiting strong zanshin, and spinning around counterclockwise. The pair will now be in opposite positions from where they started: the attacker is now on the receiving end, and vice versa.

When receiving the attacks in kirikaeshi, the receiver invites the first men attack and permits himself to be struck. He gives some resistance to the attacker's push, but allows himself to be shoved back a step. Then, as the attacker steps forward into the series of alternating men strikes, the receiver holds up his shinai so that it is in a vertical position in the center of his body. He moves the shinai slightly to meet the direction of each stroke, taking the blows on the shaft of the weapon, careful to keep it vertically aligned. In this way the shinai is moved first from to the left, then to the right as the attacks proceed. With each attack, the receiver steps backward using ayumiashi (a normal stride) and alternating steps. In this way, as the attacker steps forward into the series of four strikes, the receiver steps back with his left foot and parries to his left with the shinai. With the next attack, he steps back with his right foot and parries right, and so on.

After four steps back, the receiver steps forward, right foot first, and parrying to the left, and repeats a similar pattern through the next four steps forward. At the conclusion of his forward movements, the receiver assumes chudan, again permits the attacker to strike his men, is pushed back, and begins moving backward again. After four backward and five forward steps, the receiver permits one final men strike after which he wheels counterclockwise to assume the role of attacker.

The attacker's role in this exercise is to strike with focus and spirit, utilizing the best technique possible. She should give a strong kiai. Upon attacking, the shout "men!" should be loud and vigorous and should be given with each stroke. The ideal is to use only one breath to deliver all nine (four forward and five backward) men stokes, an aerobic challenge of some measure.

The receiver's role is to step backward far enough to permit the attacker to use her best form and to deliver the blows properly. The receiver should not evade the blows, but accept them, learning in the process to gauge proper attack distance and the timing for blocking.

Kirikaeshi is extremely fast moving. Since it utilizes the basic movements of advance and retreat and the men strike, it is a time-honored method of proper training. By pairing Kendoka up, it introduces the nature of distance and timing. Finally, it is physically demanding and an excellent way to assist in the development of stamina and spirit.

Kirikaeshi is often practiced before the start of free sparring. It is also said that it is an excellent way to end a training session. After practicing basics, uchikomi, and then engaging in sparring, Kendoka are apt to be fatigued. As a result, their technique becomes sloppy. At the end of a vigorous training session, kirikaeshi can serve as a good reminder of proper form and spirit and can help to correct the bad habits that inevitably creep into spirited sparring.

FREE SPARRING/JIYU RENSHU

The contest between two swordsmen is, of course, the situation in which technique and spirit and stamina are tested. There is a subtle difference between this type of training and contest matches, however. As we train in the dojo, we need to remember that we are there to learn from our seniors and to assist our juniors. There is a test of skill inherent in free sparring, but the learning dimension must always be remembered. In the heat and exertion and excitement of sparring, it is sometimes easy to forget this fact. Certainly one measure of the maturity of a Kendoka is in how well he or she spars, that is, how well the personal drive to excel is balanced against the need to learn and to teach. This, too, is a type of zanshin. A good Kendoka is a spirited fighter, but also one who will at the same time use the opportunity provided by free sparring to advance the knowledge of Kendo in herself or others.

In practical terms, this means that seniors will not lord their skill over juniors. They will use their superior ability to elicit the best from their partners. In the same way, junior Kendoka should not grow frustrated with their inability to "score" against more skilled partners. They will rather accept this challenge and learn from their mistakes.

Both parties should remain focused on the perfection of their art. It is customary during a sparring match for the receiver to acknowledge a well-executed strike by holding the shinai in the hodoku posture and bowing slightly toward the partner.

Sankyo (front)

Sankyo (side)

This emphasis on etiquette and civility is reinforced at both the beginning and end of a sparring session. At the beginning of a sparring match, they partners face each other, separated by about twenty-two feet. The are, of course, fully dressed in bogu and each holds his shinai at his side in his left hand, tip pointing down and to the rear. The pair bow, each raises the shinai to his hip, and takes three sliding ayumiashi steps forward—right foot, left foot, right foot. As the third step comes to an end, they draw their shinai into chudan and sink down on their haunches in the *sankyo* position. Formerly, it was said that the shinai should cross in much the same way as they do when two opponents meet in the chudan position. Now, it is recommended that the shinai tips be separated by three inches or so. After assuming sankyo, the opponents rise into chudan, cross shinai tips, and begin sparring.

At the close of the match, they once again assume sankyo, swing their shinai up and back onto the left hip (as if sheathed), rise and take five steps back. Each lowers the shinai to his left side, bows, thanks the other, and leaves the practice floor or looks for another partner.

This etiquette is the same for true contest matches, although it is not customary to thank your opponent verbally at the close of a match while still in the contest area.

---

5 . THE CLOSE

The sensei will have the end of the training session announced, usually by the senior student present. At the command, the class will line up as they did at the beginning of the session, in rank order. The students kneel and, at the command *"men tori!"* remove their kote (right first) and place them palm down, side by side, in front of and slightly to the right of their right knee. They take off the men, place it face down on the kote, putting the cords neatly inside the helmet, and remove the tenegui and drape it over the men. The equipment is then placed a bit further forward in a straight line, aligned with the equipment of the most senior student.

At this point it is customary for the sensei to comment on training, make announcements, etc. After this, some dojo will recite various pledges or *dojo kun*.

After this, the dojo captain will give the command, *"moku so!"* and the students will adopt the same meditation posture as at the beginning of the session. At *"yame!"* the meditation ends. At the command *"shomen ni, rei!"* all bow to the shomen. At *"sensei ni, rei!"* the class bows to the sensei. At *"otaga ni rei"* the class bows in unison and says *"domo arigato goziemashita,"* thanking each other for the honor of practicing together. The dojo captain announces *"kai san,"* and the lesson is over.

FIRE

Musashi describes fighting as fire. It is easy to understand why. The heat of exertion, the additional fuel of emotion, the burn of effort are all elements in the crucible of a match between swordsmen. Martial arts training has been described by the Japanese as *seishin tanren*, spiritual forging. The act of forging takes on many aspects. Discipline. Effort. Attention to detail. But nowhere does the essential nature of budo reveal itself as fully as in the act of a shiai, or match.

In the clash of free fighting, the Kendoka displays the way in which he or she has absorbed the technique and spirit of Kendo. In the dynamic swirl and attack of a Kendo match, each student of the art strives to meld spirit, technique and zanshin into each action, creating an effective and beautiful display of the art of the sword.

There are various types of contests in Kendo, some formal, some informal. During most practice sessions, students will engage in informal matches known as *keiko* or *kumite*. Here, the novice swordsman begins to put into action the basic lessons learned. Donning the bogu and engaging in practice matches, the trainee soon comes to understand how the dynamic experience of free fighting serves as an effective way to test the extent to which basic lessons have been learned. The master swordsmen who assisted in the development of Kendo were, in fact, very aware of this fact. The whole reason for the development of the shinai and bogu was to permit trainees to engage in matches without the fear of serious injury. While suburi and uchikomi are excellent training methods, as is the practice of kata, they are not in themselves complete methods of training. If Kendo is, after all, a type of fighting, then it stands to reason that part of serious training must include fighting. Kendoka practice keiko during training sessions, and must engage in more formal matches known as shiai for promotion, as well as in tournaments.

Various types of contests, then, have become an integral part of Kendo's practice throughout the world. In its emphasis on this aspect of practice, Kendo shares a perspective with judo, where *randori* is emphasized, as are tournament matches. Like judo, Kendo sometimes overemphasizes the importance of contests and tournaments, leading to a type of mental disease quite common in an environment where there are "winners" and "losers," but this does not mean that the basic emphasis on contest is in error. For any serious Kendoka, the ability to engage in keiko or shiai is a basic part of the Way of the Sword.

For a student to practice kumite, she must first have demonstrated a basic knowledge of Kendo's techniques as discussed in Part Two, Water.

Now, the trainee will once again be concerned with these matters, but will also be focused on integrating them with other considerations. While it is important in kumite to exhibit good technique, the exercise is made more challenging by the dynamic nature of movement in a match and the complications created by psychological factors (fear, overconfidence, anticipation, loss of concentration). In fact, once questions of technique and elements such as distance and timing have been successfully grappled with, the Kendoka is likely to find that the mental dimension to kumite is by far the greatest hurdle to mastery of the art.

1 . DISTANCE

One of the most elemental considerations in sparring is that of distance.

Ma-ai, or distance, refers to the ability of a Kendoka to effectively gauge the space between two opponents, and to judge when the interval is right for launching an attack, and when it places the trainee in danger of attack. Especially for beginners, it is quite common to think that you need to be much closer to launch an attack than you really do. Trainees who have studied empty-handed arts before studying Kendo, for instance, have developed a sense of distance that does not take into account the fact that the shinai is over three feet long and considerably extends the reach of the human arm. Only through practice will the Kendoka come to realize that, even if the opponent is five feet away, she is able to strike.

A solid grasp of distance is essential in Kendo. The Yagyu family of swordsmen had a saying that "the difference between living and dying lies in inches" which indicates that a good feel for ma-ai is indispensable for the swordsman.

You must constantly check the space between you and your opponent. Be sensitive to the action of the point of the shinai: as the point at which you cross weapons with your opponent slides farther down the shaft of the shinai, the danger increases. Proper distance will permit you enough time to respond to the driving attack of your opponent. If you permit yourself to be brought too near, the lightning-fast snap of your opponent's shinai will not give you enough time to react.

Paired exercises

In terms of distance, there are three locations where you can be. One is too far away for your opponent to effectively strike you—*to-ma*. In to-ma, Kendoka must step forward to bring themselves into an effective range for striking.

Issoku-itto no ma is literally the distance from which a stroke can be executed with one step forward. This is the position you take with a partner when you come into chudan for sparring. It is also known as *uchima*, or stroke interval. This is the basic interval the beginner will adopt.

The last is known as *chika-ma*, "inside" the striking distance. At this point, the Kendoka are close enough to strike without a step. Consequently, this is a position of some danger. When in chika-ma, the Kendoka must strike, move in closer so that the opponent cannot get a clean strike (often coming in so close as to push against the opponent's tsuba or hand guard, in the position known as *tsuba zerai*), or move back to get out of range.

Remember that for a stroke to score in Kendo, it must be made with the top third of the shinai, between the nakayuki and the kissaki. Consequently, an awareness of distance is vital.

---

2 . T I M I N G

Timing is another critical variable. The reason that technique is practiced so assiduously in Kendo is to make movements almost instinctive. Thinking (in the normal way we describe it) about what you will do in a match will invariably slow you down. Certainly, trying to plan a response to your opponent's action is futile. If you anticipate acting in such a way against such a technique and the opponent does not execute that technique, your plan has failed—it would only work against what you thought would happen, not against what actually transpired. If you have to think about what you will do at the moment an opponent launches a strike, your response will be too slow.

This effect, in which the mind slows things down, was called "sticking" by the Zen monk Takuan. He wrote a famous essay to the master swordsman Yagyu Munenori on the relationship between the sword and the mind. As a Zen priest, Takuan was interested in showing how our mental processes sometime interfere with our direct perception of reality. Munenori, while interested in Zen, was also a master swordsman who was fascinated by the ways in which Zen could help his sword technique. He came to the conclusion that the "Zen mind," the mizu-no-kokoro mentioned in Part Two, could assist swordsmen. Since in this state the mind is not fettered with anticipation or fear, it creates no advance plans of response and is not even consciously involved in the swordsman's actions. The opponent's sword moves, and you respond. There is no intervening mental process, and therefore the technique has the celerity needed for free fighting.

Although you should try not to anticipate too much, it is possible to become aware of patterns in your opponent's actions. In the give and take of a match, you should try to watch for these patterns in your partner's technique. Particularly under the type of stress caused by combat (even mock combat), people often fall into familiar patterns of doing things. Sparring in Kendo is no exception. A swordsman who has a favorite combination technique will tend to use it repeatedly. He will exhibit a certain rhythm in terms of how he launches techniques. If you notice such a pattern, be alive to the possibilities it presents. If you can predict your opponent's actions, you can more effectively forestall them. A word of caution, however. Advanced swordsmen, sensitive to the messages sent by timing, can set an unwary opponent up by exhibiting a pattern often enough for it to be noticed, and then taking advantage of their opponent's expectations.

3 . ATTACK AND DEFENSE

Kendo is a relentlessly offensive art: it is predicated on a strong spirit that impels the Kendoka to attack with full commitment and a feeling that he or she is so focused on the task at hand that there is no fear of receiving a blow from the opponent. Keiko should always be practiced in this spirit.

At the same time, there are a variety of ways in which this spirit can be manifest. There are times when the Kendoka will receive an attack from her opponent. The trick here is not to simply shrink back, or dodge, or block the stroke, but to attempt to transform that action into an opportunity for her own attack. In this way, even defensive motions in Kendo should never be performed in isolation, but with the intent of moving right into an attack.

Sparring

With this in mind, there are three primary opportunities for attack. *Sen*, or attack initiative, can be taken before the opponent has launched an attack (*sen-no-sen*). A Kendoka may launch a strike as the opponent begins an attack (sen), forestalling the success of the opponent's move through a variety of strategies. Finally, the Kendoka may counter an attack and launch an attack of her own through *go-no-sen*.

Each of these responses is built upon the combination of sound timing and technique. They also make use of the effect of the mind on human action. In sen-no-sen, the Kendoka strikes before the opponent has a chance to move. At this juncture, the opponent's spirit and mind are focused on gathering energy for the attack. For a split second, the opponent is focused on preparing for the attack, which means that attention is not as well focused on the other Kendoka. She attacks.

In sen, quickness in action and precision act to forestall an attack. Here, the opponent's focus is on the attack. He launches a stroke and she quickly acts to respond. Particularly in less experienced Kendoka, the process of attacking creates openings for a counter—coming in to strike men, for example, often gives the opportunity to counter with a kote strike.

In a go-no-sen situation, the Kendoka negates the attack through a variety of stratagems and then counters with one of her own. At this juncture, the opponent's mind "pauses" briefly. It has been focused on the launching of a strike and, at its completion, must shift focus. At this juncture, there is an opening that can be exploited.

The novice should be cautioned, however, that "pauses" and "gaps" in Kendo are extremely brief, particularly when you are faced with a skilled opponent. It is frequently the case that the beginner will experience an awareness of an opportunity—"Aha! Now I can counter kote!"—only to see the chance disappear in the time it took to recognize it. Only time and experience can develop the skill needed to practice Kendo on this more advanced level. For beginners, it is best to focus on a simple, straightforward approach to keiko.

ATTACKS/SHIKAKE WAZA

Shikake waza are essentially offensive techniques—they are launched when the Kendoka sees an opportunity. These are fundamental techniques that beginners should focus on.

Multiple Attacks/Nidan and Sandan Waza

In uchikomi, the Kendoka is familiar with the launching of various strikes—men, kote, do, and tsuki. Such techniques are important for fostering spirit. In keiko, however, it is rare that a single-step technique results in a point. Combining strikes in a multiple attack is a very effective way of causing your opponent to react and so create an opening.

In the combination of kote-men, the Kendoka attacks with a feint to the kote. If the opponent lowers the shinai or withdraws his fists slightly, a opening has been created for the Kendoka to strike men.

If the Kendoka feints to kote again, and the opponent raises his fists in response, then an opening has been created for a strike to do.

Finally, if the Kendoka attacks men, and the opponent raises his fists in response, the opportunity has presented itself for a do attack.

These are just three common examples of a multiple attack. These techniques work by causing your opponent to create an opening through his reactions to what he thinks you are doing. Hence, in two- or three-step techniques, the initial moves are truly feints—they are intended to make your opponent move into a disadvantageous position—and the final technique is the action that should be strongly executed with good spirit and follow-through.

The reader will also notice that multiple-attack techniques cannot be fully planned before they are launched—depending upon your opponent's reaction, your second or third technique will vary. Only practice and experience can assist in the development of strong and effective multiple attacks.

Warding Off Attack/Harai Waza

Another sen-no-sen attack involves using the upward swing of the shinai as you attack, as a way of warding off your opponent's shinai and creating an opening.

When engaged in issoku-itto no ma, a successful technique much be launched quickly. If your opponent presents a strong kamae, however, an opening may not present itself. To purposefully knock the opponent's shinai aside, however, could conceivably open you up to an attack. In Kendo there is always an emphasis on efficiency and economy of movement. *Harai waza* demonstrate this by using the upward movement of the shinai as the Kendoka prepares to attack: the move up slightly displaces the opponent's shinai at the same time that it places the Kendoka's weapon in the precise position needed for attack. Harai waza can have varied targets as the opportunity presents itself.

Forestalling Attack/Debana Waza

Debana waza are a good illustration of the sen attack. In these techniques, you launch a strike just as the opponent begins a move. The opening presented lasts only a split second, so technique in debana waza must be quick. As a result, debana waza are relatively "small" techniques.

What this means is that, instead of raising the arms fully and bringing the shinai overhead, as in the standard form practiced in suburi and uchikomi, the Kendoka extends his arms toward the opponent as he moves in and uses the wrists to snap a stroke at a target.

For instance, as the opponent begins to move forward you will very often notice that the tip of the shinai bobs down slightly. At just this moment, the Kendoka should launch debana-men to take advantage of the lowered guard and make a men point. In the same way, if an opponent raises his fists in preparation for a strong men attack, the Kendoka delivers debana-kote.

A successful debana waza hinges on speed of delivery and precision as well as on the ability to recognize an opening as it develops.

RECEIVING TECHNIQUES/OJI WAZA

The ideal in Kendo is to be always on the attack. In reality, however, this is not really possible. One of the most humbling things about Kendo is that, no matter how good you become, there is always someone better. In addition, we all have weaknesses, expose gaps, and have days when our mind "sticks." As a result, all Kendoka can expect to be on the receiving end of attacks.

This is not a negative thing, however. Part of the rationale for training in Kendo is to develop the ability to persevere in adversity. The point of engaging in contest matches is not just to show how well you can strike others. It is also to show how well you react when others strike you: how resolute your spirit remains, how you respond in counterattack, how well you maintain your composure when things are not going your way. If Kendo training is in part a way to train you for life, it would be a glaring omission if it did not include an opportunity to learn how to deal with problems as well as successes.

In this regard, *oji waza* are ways for the Kendoka to cope with attacks and turn them to her advantage.

Dodging/Nuki Waza

One of the most natural reactions to an attack is evasion. *Nuki waza* are dodges of a sort, but dodges with a difference. In Kendo, you should maintain a spirit that does not flinch. As a result, to dodge an attack merely to escape being hit is considered poor form. In addition, such haste to avoid being hit often breaks your posture and prevents you from countering effectively. In Kendo, we seek to dodge in order to have the opponent beat the air instead of strike us and at the same time put ourselves in a position to counter immediately.

The first two Kendo kata (see Part Four, Wind) are essentially exercises in nuki waza. In the first kata, the attacker strikes men. The defender steps back half a step to dodge the blow and then comes forward to counter men. In the second kata, the attacker attempts a kote strike. The defender steps obliquely left, lowers his sword to evade, then brings it up to strike kote. Another example is stepping in obliquely to your right as the opponent launches a men attack and countering do.

These three examples stress the idea that the dodge is designed to bring you into a position to attack, not merely escape from a strike. Therefore, the emphasis must not be on the movement of evasion, but on the subsequent attack. The feeling in nuki waza is not "DODGE!-strike," but rather "dodge-STRIKE!" The Kendoka needs to be careful in the use of nuki waza. It is a human impulse to avoid attack. In Kendo, we harness that impulse in order to enable us to counter an assault. In this way, we bring both our "flight and fight" impulses to bear on the situation.

Parries

As the trainee becomes more skilled in the use of the shinai, she will be able to use it in a variety of quick and subtle actions that will considerably assist in the delivery of strikes. These actions can be subsumed under the heading of *parries*. In Kendo, parries are executed in three directions: up, down, and to the side. It should be noted that it is often quite effective to incorporate a rotary motion of the shinai tip into the parries: the force of such a movement can sometimes wrench the shinai right out of the hands of the unwary opponent.

Up Parry/Suriage Waza

Suriage waza uses the upward swing of the Kendoka's shinai to parry an opponent's attack at the same time that it brings the Kendoka's weapon into a position to strike. It is similar to harai waza, but is a reflexive move that is made in reaction to an attack rather than one that is initiated before the opponent moves.

An example of suriage waza is presented in the fifth kata (see Part Four, Wind), which demonstrates men-suriage-men. The attacker initiates a men strike. The defender swings his sword up into jodan no kamae. In doing so, he strikes the attacker's defending sword up and off center so that the cut is ineffectual. The defender then counters with a men strike.

The important point in suriage waza is to incorporate the parry into the motion of raising the shinai so that one motion serves two purposes. In this way defense and attack become blended in one movement.

Downward Parry/Uchiotoshi Waza

The attacker's shinai may be parried down as well. This is not seen as often as suriage waza, and the Kendoka needs to be cautious so that the attempt at a downward parry does not bring his own shinai so far down and off-center that it inhibits the ability to strike the opponent.

The clearest illustration of this technique occurs when the opponent attempts to strike the Kendoka's right do. By shifting the fists to the right, the Kendoka can parry the stroke down and to the side and leave his shinai to rise up and strike the opponent's men.

Lateral Parry/Kaeshi Waza

Kaeshi waza use the force of an attack to propel the counter. The Kendoka receives the blow on his shinai, then uses the reflexive force to bring his shinai back, forcing the opponent's shinai off-center and presenting the opportunity for a counter.

CLOSE QUARTERS/TSUBA-ZERAI

Since Kendo's emphasis is on attack, it is not unusual for Kendoka to come to close quarters as one or the other attempts to follow through on an unsuccessful attack. In such cases, it is important for the trainee to keep his fists centered and the shinai held up and slightly to the right. Push in with the handle of the shinai held at chest height so that the shafts of the two shinai meet just above the tsuba. At this juncture, neither contestant can deliver a clean blow: it is analogous to clinching in boxing.

Tsuba-zerai
(close up)

Tsuba-zerai
(full figure)

As in boxing, this position is not one you should linger in. In the spirit of Kendo, if you close, it is with the purpose of launching a successful attack. If the force of your follow-through brings you to *tsuba zerai,* you should use this as a stepping-off point for a new attack.

Pushing-Off Attack/Hiki Waza

Opponents in *hiki waza* clinch to test each other's spirit. They push to see if one can cause the other to lose his balance or reveal a gap in defensive posture. By pushing against the opponent's fists with his own, the Kendoka can sometimes cause the opponent to either raise or lower his guard. At that moment, the Kendoka can step back and deliver a strike to the appropriate target.

For example, if the opponent lowers his guard, the Kendoka steps back and delivers a men strike.

It should be noted that in practice it is difficult to score such a strike cleanly in contest. You must spring back into a stable stance, raise your shinai up so that its tip points forty-five degrees to the rear, strike the men clearly, and then bring the shinai back into the forty-five degree position in a strong jodan no kamae while moving backward. Hiki waza demonstrate good spirit, however, and the ability to transform a disadvantageous position into an opportunity for attack, and so should be practiced frequently.

ZANSHIN

In the excitement of keiko, it is often easy to slip into bad habits in terms of technique. Kendo masters seek to remind students of this by insisting on the demonstration of zanshin in matches. Zanshin literally means "remaining mind" and, like many Japanese philosophical terms, has a number of different interpretations, depending on the situation. For Kendoka, zanshin refers to a type of follow-through that exhibits focus, good technique, and emotive control, even in the heat of a contest. Without a good demonstration of zanshin, the Kendoka will not be awarded a point in a match, no matter how many times she hits her opponent.

When the Kendoka strikes, he should do so with a sense of full commitment. When a strike is made properly, the trainee should follow through by moving past the opponent with the shinai held in the appropriate manner and with strong posture. Then the Kendoka should wheel around and face the opponent, ready to deal with any move. If you are moving backwards while striking, you must also exhibit strong zanshin. If you are striking men, zanshin is demonstrated in the manner described in the part on hiki waza.

SPIRIT

It is important to realize that, despite all the discussion of technique and strategy, Kendo is primarily a thing of the spirit. A match is an opportunity to demonstrate the strength of the human spirit through the practice of this art. To a large extent, it is not even important whether you score points or emerge victorious in a match. What is important is that you attempt, to the utmost of your ability, to perform Kendo in a way that does credit to your teachers.

This spirit is demonstrated in a number of ways. A strong kiai is important, as is the shout used as you attack a particular target. Your stance and movements should be precise. You must demonstrate zanshin. Finally, it is important to demonstrate respect to all present: senior

Kendoka, judges, opponents, and other trainees. Whatever the outcome of a match, the trainee should always be in control of his emotions. Demonstrations of anger, disappointment, or even elation are considered bad form. The Kendoka should always keep in mind the fact that the contest is designed not for the defeat or aggrandizement of individuals, but to refine and develop the art of the sword as it is practiced by Kendoka around the world.

4. THE SHIAI

Shiai are the formal gatherings used to test individuals for advancement in rank and for tournament purposes. Not every Kendoka will be a strong tournament player. All Kendoka can benefit, however, from the experience of crossing shinai with new individuals, from watching the technique of others and from the opportunities presented to learn from high ranking sensei.

In essence a shiai is little different from the keiko of normal practice, although it if performed with a great deal more formality. In addition, the presence of judges, a time limit, and the keeping of score make this experience somewhat different.

The contest area's dimensions are established by regulation. It is between 9 and 11 meters square, and its boundaries are clearly marked by a white line 5 to 10 centimeters wide. The exact center of the square is marked, as are two point each exactly 1.5 meters from the center. These starting marks are where the contestant will line up. They are 1 meter long.

In shiai, there is often a table of high-ranking Kendoka watching the proceedings from one side of the square. In addition, there are three judges or *shimpan*—two forward and one rear. There are also two individuals placed at opposite corners to check to see whether a contestant steps out of bounds.

In shiai, each contestant is identified with a piece of red or white cloth tied to the do strings that cross behind their backs. The two forward shimpan carry a small flag in each hand—one red and one white. They signal the scoring of a point by raising the appropriate flag. Both judges must agree that a stroke has scored cleanly for it to count. If one judge raises a flag but the other disagrees, the point is nullified by the shimpan lowering both flags in front and crossing them.

Contestants stand on opposite sides of the square outside its boundaries. At a signal from the judges, they step in, bow, and take three ayumiashi steps to the center. They assume sankyo, draw their shinai, stand, and assume chudan.

At the command *"Hajime!"* the match begins. The judges manage the flow of the contest. If they must pause the contest for some reason, they will give the command *"Yame!"*

Kendoka vie to score the best of three points by striking the normal target areas of Kendo. The match usually lasts for no more than five minutes. If time runs out before either contestant scores two points, the judges will announce *"Encho,"* and the match will continue.

Contestants must remain within the boundaries of the square. If a Kendoka inadvertently steps out, he is given a warning. When he does so a second time, it is a point counted against him. If a Kendoka steps out of bounds, the judge calls *"Yame! Moto no ichi ni kaere!"* which is the command to halt and return to the original position.

When the match is over, the judges call "Yame" and signal to the winner with the appropriate color flag. The contestants return to the center, assume sankyo, place their shinai at their left hips, stand, and step back five small steps, where they bow before stepping out of the square.

THE PSYCHODYNAMICS OF COMPETITION

As I have indicated, there is a significant mental dimension to competition. Kendo's masters included a competitive emphasis for just this reason. By combining the psychic stresses involved in questions of triumph and defeat with the physical challenges of the art, they have made Kendo a uniquely challenging experience for even the most skilled player and the most balanced human being. For this reason, trainees are wise to reflect on the proper mental attitude necessary to fully benefit from the shiai experience and to acknowledge some of the common pitfalls individuals face.

Pride

When we engage in martial arts training, we are investing considerable time and energy in an enterprise intensely concerned with image: that which we hold for ourselves and that which we create about ourselves for others. In donning the uniform and armor of a Kendo trainee, we, in effect, take on an enhanced personality. We make a statement about who we are and what we would like to be capable of doing. In this sense, Kendo training can assist us in the development of a healthy type of self-esteem: one built on accomplishment and the resolute meeting of significant challenges.

Shiai, in a sense, pose a challenge to that self-image. A contest is, in some ways, a public judgment on our skills and our fortitude. After all, in each match, there is a winner and a loser. This creates a situation in which our self-image and esteem is put to the test in a very dramatic way. Shiai forces us to "put our money where our mouth is" and demonstrate the depth of our acquisition of Kendo's skills.

In reality, we cannot realistically expect to emerge victorious every time we engage in a contest. For some trainees, this is a hard fact to accept. And yet such an acknowledgment is an integral part of the process of spiritual maturation.

Men strike

So in a sense, the Kendo masters were very clever in requiring a con-test emphasis. This is a significant challenge on both physical and psy-chological levels for trainees. It tests the level of skill development at the same time that it serves as a humbling reminder of personal limitations and as a check on the development of a type of false pride.

Anger and Excitement

There is something about being enmeshed in a competitive activity that rouses the emotions. In Kendo, we seek to harness the emotive response of a human being to assist in creating forceful technique. The flight or fight mechanism that provides a biological basis for quick and forceful action can help us in a Kendo match. Certainly part of the function of the shouts used in Kendo is to express spirit or intimidate the opponent, but it also probably has the effect of creating a physical reaction on the part of the individual giving the shout. There is a real link between emotional states and physical capabilities.

Yet we need to be cautious about our emotions. We need to use them, not have them take control of us.

One of the most significant emotions we need to control is anger. In a situation where you are being bested by an opponent, it is all too easy to surrender to a type of resentment and frustration. This, in turn, leads the individual to lose a certain amount of control of his or her actions. When we permit ourselves to grow discouraged or angry, we lose the focus that Kendo demands. As a result, our technique suffers. It is not unusual to see frustrated contestants whacking away at each other in a frenzy, trying to score a point. In such a situation, their emotions have caused their technique to deteriorate to such a point that it is highly unlikely that the judges will determine that a proper strike has been executed. The question of bad technique is only a minor point; the display of any kind of anger or frustration in a shiai is a demonstration of how poorly the individual in question has been able to internalize the spirit of Kendo.

Winning and Losing

From my perspective, the greatest impediment to developing good Kendo is an overemphasis on winning and losing. Contests should be engaged in with vigor and enthusiasm. But, at the same time, Kendoka need to keep in mind the ultimate purpose of training (and, to my mind, shiai is a type of training): the development of the human spirit through the medium of Kendo.

It is easy to fall into the trap of caring too much about whether you are scoring or not, even in informal matches. Particularly in the early periods of your apprenticeship, it becomes wearing to be struck so often and to be unable to strike back in return. As a result, beginners will attempt to cut corners in their technique as a way to obtain more speed. Anyone who watches some tournament players will note the difference between the "orthodox" method of striking and the "tournament" version. In competition, Kendoka often do not use the full swing of the suburi motion to strike, instead relying on "small" techniques that can be launched quickly. When properly used, these can be quite effective. The danger for beginners, however, is that they may adopt these "small" techniques and never master the underpinnings of classic Kendo technique. As a result, they will be able to obtain some success in competitive situations but, ultimately, will never progress beyond a certain point.

The best attitude to take in sparring, as in all training, is one that does not focus on what others are doing around you or to you, but rather on how you are emulating the techniques shown to you by the sensei. Get used to the idea that you will be hit quite frequently in a sparring match. There is nothing wrong with this; it is not some sort of sign of "failure." There is, after all, a reason why Kendoka wear armor.

Try to always execute technique fully, whether it is successful against an opponent or not. You will find that training this way is extremely challenging: I have found that, in the beginning stages, it is a far harder workout if you concentrate on executing strikes and not opt for the "small" techniques and easy victories they promise.

Kiri kaeshi

Remember: in Kendo, a fidelity to tradition and the spirit with which you train are as important (if not more so) than your contest skill. Even in the examinations for lower dan ranks, judges are more interested in technique and technical competence than they are in tournament success. Not everyone, after all, can be a Kendo champion. We can all strive, however, to mirror something of Kendo's spirit in the way we go about its practice.

My favorite story in this regard centers around the conversation a bunch of American Kendoka were having with a Japanese champion. The Americans had just been treated to a display of lighting-fast, truly breathtaking Kendo by the champion. After practice, they were eager to talk with him to see whether they could pick up some training tips. It turned out he had only one thing to offer them as advice: to make your Kendo effective, you must first make it beautiful.

Even in the heat of competition, we need to remember this.

PART FOUR

WIND

In the portion of the *Book of Five Rings* titled "Wind," Musashi likens this element to the patterns and practices of other schools of swordsmanship. Throughout the world, people have used the wind as a metaphor to communicate something of the mysterious creative power in nature and the impact of the unseen upon our lives. In this sense, we can envision how the energies, insights, and experiences of martial artists linked together in the tradition of the sword continue to reverberate down the long corridor of the centuries. Kendo is built upon the currents of tradition created by these generations of swordsmen, and so its origins and influences are worth exploring.

1. TRADITION

The suffix "do" in Kendo and other modern martial arts such as judo, iaido, and aikido, literally means "way" or "path." Hence, Kendo is the "way of the sword." A way in its broadest sense is a route from one place to another. When we train in Kendo, we are participating in a type of human experience with roots deep in Japanese history and culture.

We are also treading a path that stretches on before us into the future. Kendo, as a human endeavor, is an ever-evolving art. Each Kendoka steps along the path, and the process should assist in helping us to remember where this path has been, as well as contribute something toward its ultimate destination.

Kendo has its roots in the Japanese historical experience. Certainly its trappings, customs, and philosophy reflect this. At the same time, trainees should be cautious in thinking about themselves as the heirs of the art of the samurai in the technical sense. It is quite common today to see various arts touted as "samurai" this or "samurai" that. Such claims may, at best, be a type of wishful thinking. If not, they represent the claims of individuals whose ignorance of the development of the martial arts has led them to a fairly serious error. We may well advocate the position that Kendo creates a type of link with the experience of past swordsmen, but, as we shall see, it is a link of a particular type.

It seems to me that part of the obligation a trainee has in honoring and respecting Kendo is learning many things about this art. This includes an honest assessment of Kendo's strengths and weaknesses, its heritage, its evolution, and its potential for practitioners today. In this way, students will come to a clearer understanding about what Kendo truly is and also be able to pass this knowledge on to others. Part of the way this is done is through physical means, and this is accomplished through the type of practice we have discussed in previous chapters. In addition, Kendoka need to study the Kendo no kata, Kendo's formal exercises, which have been designed to embody significant techniques and lessons culled from a variety of the most famous styles of swordsmanship that survived into the twentieth century.

---

2 . HISTORICAL DEVELOPMENT

Kendo is the most respected form of the martial arts in modern Japan, most likely because, as a derivative of feudal sword arts, it is thought of as having tangible links to the samurai. Like most modern martial arts, Kendo can be thought of as a ritualized, sportive version of Japanese combat systems. I say it is "ritualized" because, due to the modifications made to it, Kendo is not a true "combat art." It has evolved from combat arts of the past, but it has done so in a special way. Kendo has preserved the mental and physical stresses of fighting, but has done so in a system that eliminates the mortal danger of combat. Its function is not, therefore, to teach trainees how to kill with the sword. On the contrary, Kendo's philosophy is one that seeks to enhance, not destroy, life.

Going to the opposite extreme and characterizing Kendo as a form of recreation, pure and simple, however, is equally erroneous. Kendo is not just a sport.

The Way of the Sword is the contemporary heir of a broad spectrum of Japanese cultural influences that were embedded in the martial traditions of feudal warriors. For this reason, Kendo is considered by serious practitioners to be something more than just a form of exercise or competition; it approaches a type of spiritual discipline.

In other words, Kendo is fairly complex on a number of levels.

Since Kendo is based on the use of the Japanese sword, we can look for the start of its evolutionary process during the Nara period (710–794). The oldest swords in Japan date from the second century B.C., but it was not until the eighth century A.D. that the first models of what would become the distinctive single-edged, curved Japanese sword known as the katana emerged.

Swords, of course, were made to be used. In the centuries that followed the Nara period, a social class of armed fighting men known as samurai developed and eventually came to play a dominant role in Japanese social and political life. Particularly in later centuries, not all members of the samurai class were warriors (bushi), but this portion of Japanese society was defined by its role as a group of combat specialists.

The samurai developed a wide variety of armed and unarmed fighting techniques. The use of the bow and arrow, the spear, halberds, and pole-arms of various sorts was all grist for the warrior's mill. They were also students of unarmed grappling. Since the samurai typically fought in armor, however, these grappling techniques were substantially different from the later methods developed as *jujutsu*. In addition, as professional fighters everywhere acknowledge, unarmed fighting is difficult and dangerous. Combat without a weapon is the last resort of desperate men. The samurai far preferred to enter the battlefield armed and in armor.

This difference in emphasis and technique between "classic" samurai combat forms—normally labeled as *jutsu*—and modern systems—shin budo—is an important point to note. In the same way that unarmed systems today are different from their feudal prototypes, modern weapon systems differ as well.

The samurai were proficient in a wide variety of weapons. But pride of place was occupied by the two-handed slashing sword, the katana. It was a work of deadly efficiency as well as breathtaking beauty. Its long, curved blade held a single razor-sharp edge, the result of a unique forging method that embedded a brittle, highly sharpened edge into a more flexible main body that lent the sword resilience.

Samurai typically wore two swords—known as *daisho*—thrust into the left side of their sash, blades facing up. One sword, the longer of the two, was the katana, or *tachi*. The second, a shorter blade, was known as the *wakizashi* or *kodachi*. The katana was typically drawn in a slashing "sky to ground" technique. The short sword was typically used in close-quarter grappling, especially if the katana was lost or broken in the heat of battle. In later years, perhaps under the influence of Portuguese and other European fencers, some swordsmen used both swords at once. Miyamoto Musashi was perhaps the most famous exponent of the two-sword technique and, even today, it is not unusual to see Kendoka training in the *nito* (two sword) style.

The samurai honed their combat techniques over centuries of combat waged in the narrow mountain valleys of Japan's islands, on the coast repelling Mongol invaders, and in the Korean peninsula. But we have no evidence of any real systematized methods of practice until the Muromachi period (1392–1573).

A watershed in Japanese history for the art of the sword is marked by the life of Izasa Choisai Ienao (1387-1488), the founder of the Tenshin Shoden Katori Shinto Ryu of swordsmanship. He was a man gifted with both skill in arms and an analytical mind. Choisai founded his *ryu* (style) after a period of fasting, meditation, and training that lasted one thousand days. His style of kenjutsu (sword techniques) was a precise, rigorous system that regulated all phases of swordplay, from physical preparation and technique to mental attitude. His style is the oldest ryu of which we have historical documentation, and its organization and sophistication set the style for subsequent schools of swordsmanship. Considering the bellicose nature of Japan's history during the two centuries following Choisai's death, there was ample opportunity and motivation for the evolution of other ryu of swordsmanship.

The period following the Onin War (1467–1477) witnessed both technical systematization and ideological elaboration concerning the arts of the sword. By the Tokugawa period (1600–1868), hundreds of martial arts styles had developed, although in a sense they can all be seen as developing from a few main traditions.

The structure of these schools or styles of swordsmanship was affected by the social and political organization of the time. Ryu were hierarchical organizations, with a great stress on rank and status. At the head of this organization was the master, who either founded the ryu, building on his own skill and insight, or inherited the mantle of leadership by virtue of his position as a disciple of the ryu's head. In the days when samurai were actively engaged in combat, the various techniques passed on from master to disciple could spell the difference between life and death. Training was conducted with the utmost seriousness and commitment, and the secrets of a ryu's technique were jealously guarded.

Despite a widespread belief that the samurai were "Zen warriors," Japanese culture is a religiously eclectic environment, teeming with spirits and forces and beliefs. The establishment of many ryu was often attributed to a flash of spiritual inspiration bestowed on the founder. Because of this element of supernatural inspiration, ryu were often associated with Shinto shrines and were considered to be protected by the power inherent in these locations.

The belief that these ryu were inspired in the religious sense led to the tradition of the transmission of a school's secrets from master to disciple through direct teaching and the legacy of *makimono*, or hand scrolls. Although written guides, these scrolls, which recorded the strategy, techniques, and insights of the ryu, are rather vague and purposefully cryptic. As a result, they were generally understandable only by initiates. *Go Rin No Sho* is an example of this type of scroll. Although it has many concrete lessons it can give us, certainly some of its more oblique and poetic references could only be fully grasped by Musashi's disciples.

Training in swordsmanship usually centered around the use of the bokken, or wooden training sword, in basic exercises as well as in the paired drills known as kata. Kata are familiar to many martial artists as routines that embody significant techniques for trainees. In feudal Japan, the razor-sharp katana was both too fragile and too dangerous to be used in practice of a nonlethal sort. As a result, training implements of wood were used. They were durable and could be fashioned to mimic the balance and heft of real weapons, but they were not invariably lethal. At the same time, however, a hard wooden sword could inflict substantial injuries. As a result, despite its relative safety, it could elicit considerable respect from trainees and create a properly serious frame of mind during kata practice.

The ultimate test of fighting ability in the feudal era was, of course, combat. The next best thing, however, was kata. Paired kata with hard wooden weapons is a demanding and potentially dangerous activity. Some modern martial artists disparage kata as empty "dancing." This would suggest that they have never really "seen" kata.

Traditional kata were designed to teach trainees lessons their masters had learned on the battlefield. They were the distillation of literally decades of experience. In feudal Japan, a sensei taught his students kata that embodied lessons he had learned, often at the expense of another's life. They were not meant to be empty performances. They were the absolutely vital remembrance of the things a warrior needed to know before he entered a real battlefield.

Until the seventeenth century, the way of the sword could, at least theoretically, be described as one concerned and with the application of these skills through practice training with the bokken and application in combat with the live blade of the katana. As the Tokugawa shogunate unified Japan and put an end to centuries of warfare, however, the military utility of the swordsman waned. Despite this, the Japanese continued to value training in swordsmanship, seeing it as a badge of social honor and as a method of personal refinement.

In an age when a samurai's utility to his lord was no longer judged by his ferocity, but by his more enduring peaceful service, there eventually grew a need for safer methods of practice. At the same time, sensei recognized that there was a virtue in experiencing the tension, speed, and danger of a combat situation. To permit a simulation of such combat, they developed armor (today's bogu) and a special implement to take the place of the deadly katana. Thus the need to reduce the chance of training injuries, which had earlier given rise to the use of the bokken, eventually resulted in the creation of the shinai (bamboo fencing foil) during the eighteenth century. Various swordsmen had experimented with different types of shinai since at least the sixteenth century—the Shin-Kage and Yagyu Shin-Kage Ryu used a suede-bound bundle of bamboo that inspired the implement known as a *fukoro* shinai, still seen today in some aikido schools. Eventually, the prototype of today's shinai evolved—four pieces of split bamboo bound together with leather at the tip and the handle. This implement is not really shaped like a katana (it is not curved). It is longer (the handle is long to accommodate the mitts worn as protection). It is lighter (being made of wood). But is has the excellent quality of permitting trainees to strike each other fully and without reservation in highly energetic matches.

With this development, the evolution of the modern Way of the Sword began to bifurcate along two separate lines: Kendo, which concentrated on training with the shinai in an active, competitive environment, and iaido, which focused on practicing with the live blade in a series of formal solo exercises. At the same time, traditional systems of kenjutsu preserved the strong emphasis on kata and a combat orientation.

The modern *do* forms of swordsmanship developed in a way designed to make them accessible to a wider portion of Japanese society. Traditionalists view this development as a regrettable modification that compromises the essence of swordsmanship. In a sense, both the arts of Kendo and iaido have their merits and their disadvantages. On the plus side, Kendo's adoption of the shinai has permitted it to foster a spirited competitive dimension that mimics the challenge of the battlefield. For its part, iaido performs a positive function in that it teaches trainees how to use a real sword.

Neither art precisely preserves the traditional techniques of combat with a real weapon. Kendo's armor and shinai make for a different type of experience and for techniques different from those actually used by the samurai. Iaido's emphasis on solo forms, clashes fought in a civilian atmosphere without armor, and esthetics can also be seen as robbing it of some of the vigor and battlefield reality of a bushi's experience.

While maintaining that these two arts do, in fact, have something positive to teach us, advanced practitioners will also acknowledge that these modern arts are not "complete" in themselves. It is widely held by Kendoka, for instance, that no true understanding of the way of the sword is possible without some proficiency in iaido as well.

In addition, Kendo masters have attempted to incorporate a type of training that gives trainees some insight into the dynamics and use of the katana. The first steps in learning how to wield the sword of the samurai use the wooden practice sword in a series of paired kata. In this way, Kendo emphasizes training with the bokken as a way of developing basic skills and preserving a link with the past.

3. KATA

Kendo's kata are a link for the *kenshi* of today with the generations of swordsmen who shaped the evolution of Japanese sword arts.

The Nihon Kendo no Kata are a series of ten formal exercises practiced by Kendoka. They were developed in conference in the early twentieth century by some of the foremost swordsmen in Japan. The kata have evolved through time: revisions and reexaminations taking place in 1912, 1917, 1933, and 1981. The kata are intended to embody significant insights into the practice of Kendo in its broadest sense. As such, they bear careful study.

It must be admitted that many trainees neglect kata training. The allure and dash of sparring certainly has a strong attraction, especially for young trainees. In many ways, the situation in Kendo mirrors that in judo: a theoretically balanced system of training that includes both formal and free types of practice but that has, in reality, been selectively practiced in such a way as to erode the fuller dimension of the art. There is nothing more disheartening than seeing a dojo full of spirited free-fighters stumble their way through Kendo's forms. At the same time, there is nothing that communicates the essence of Kendo better than a finely executed kata. Kendoka, therefore, should accept the wisdom of generations of martial artists before them and fully accept kata as an important component in developing mature and skilled practitioners.

By practicing kata, trainees learn to wield a weapon much more similar in weight, shape, and dynamics to a real sword. They gain a grasp of precision in movement, presence, and composure. As a type of historical shorthand that records the key techniques of Japan's old sword styles, kata link Kendoka to their past. Finally, kata are an important opportunity for the development and demonstration of zanshin and spirit, key qualities for all followers of the Way of the Sword.

THE SPIRIT OF KATA

In kata, spirit is everything. It is easy to let kata degenerate into a mechanical exercise. This is certainly what has led many martial artists to disparage kata in many arts. But this is not true kata. The performance of a kata should be alive with tension, electric, and dynamic. It should be invested with a spirit that makes each move seem as if it were being executed for real.

And, indeed, on a certain level, it is.

When a trainee practices kata, there is a psychodynamic aspect that needs to be maintained. Although kata are, by definition, set pieces in which each move and response is known beforehand, they are choreographed versions of combat. Each attack is meant to deliver a decisive blow. Each defensive move must be executed as if the attack were driven by killing intent. In this regard, the composure and control you exhibit is as important as (if not more so than) the technique displayed. It is possible for you to stumble technically in kata demonstration and yet successfully complete the performance through the maintenance of spirit and focus.

Kata, in other words, are equally as grueling as keiko, but in a different way. Keiko shows how we cope with the rapid environment of conflict, with an emphasis on physical response. Under the microscopic examination possible during the more sedate performance of kata, we are subject to scrutiny that seeks to measure our psychic composure and focus.

THE KENDO NO KATA

There are ten kata practiced today in Kendo. Unlike the practice in karate, where forms are given symbolic names (for example, *Heian*— Heavenly Peace) or names that identify the elements such as judo's *Nage no Kata*—kata of throws), Kendo's kata are more prosaically identified by number. Kendo's kata are divided into two groups: The first seven kata are practiced using only the long sword, or tachi. In the final three, the defender uses both the long sword and the short sword, or kodachi. The names of the kata are as follows :

Ipponme—First Kata

Nihonme—Second Kata

Sanbonme—Third Kata

Yohonme—Fourth Kata

Gohonme—Fifth Kata

Ropponme—Sixth Kata

Nanahonme—Seventh Kata

Kodachi Ipponme—First Kata, using two swords

Kodachi Nihonme—Second Kata, using two swords

Kodachi Sanbonme—Third Kata, using two swords

In this section we will focus on a description of the first five kata, which are necessary for advancement to the first dan level.

Bokken

The kata are practiced using the hard wooden training sword, the bokken. As we have seen, it has a long history as a training implement in Japanese martial arts. Its value here in kata practice lies in its dynamic similarity to a real sword. Indeed, high-ranking Kendoka will sometimes demonstrate these kata using katana.

It is common in some other martial arts forms such as aikido for trainees to use bokken that are not fitted with a hand-guard or tsuba. In Kendo, the bokken are usually used with a tsuba, particularly in the later kata, since the guards are used in the execution of some techniques.

Kata are practiced without armor. During grading shiai, tare are worn for identification purposes. Given the semilethal nature of the bokken, this fact lends kata performance a dash of tension and demands rigid control and precision from the practitioners—it is possible to seriously injure someone with a bokken. As a result, when first learning kata, it is wise to exaggerate distance somewhat until proficiency is obtained in the use of the weapon.

Sage-to

When moving to and from the performance space, carry the bokken in the right hand to signify pacific intent. Hold the sword cutting edge up, with you hand on the shaft just behind the hilt, kissaki (point) pointing down and to the rear. If carrying both the long and short sword, grip the smaller one with the thumb and forefinger, the larger sword with the remaining three fingers. This position is known as *sage-to*.

Bowing In

Kendo no kata are paired exercises. The two trainees stand facing each other, about nine steps apart. In these kata, one Kendoka is designated as *uchidachi*, the aggressor in the exercise. The other is *shidachi*, who defends and ultimately gains the offensive.

The kamiza, or shomen, is at the head of the room. For purposes of our discussion, this area is to shidachi's left and uchidachi's right.

The two Kendoka stand facing each other, holding their bokken in sage-to position. They turn toward the shomen and execute a standing rei in the prescribed manner. They turn to face each other and complete a bow to each other that is less deep. They also keep their eyes on each other, signaling the state of heightened awareness necessary in the performance of kata.

On the completion of the bow, if shidachi is carrying the kodachi, he steps three steps to his right rear, kneels on his right knee, and places the kodachi down, cutting edge facing in.

He then returns to his position facing uchidachi.

At this point, the two performers transfer their bokken to their left hand, holding the sword in the prescribed manner at the left hip.

The Kendoka step in three steps, perform sankyo, and rise. They lower their swords to the hodoku position, and step back five steps. At the completion of the movement, they assume chudan no kamae.

They are now ready to perform the kata.

Stepping In and Stepping Out

You engage and disengage in the same way for each kata. Basically, it is a pattern of three large striding steps in (starting with your right foot) and five small striding steps out (starting with your left), using ayumiashi.

Coming in, you hold the bokken in the kamae appropriate for each kata. When the three steps are completed, you should be in issoku itto no ma, close enough to strike with one step forward. If you are in chudan, the bokken should cross about three inches from the tip.

Stepping back, you disengage, using the hodoku posture, bokken lowered and pointed to the right. Step back first with your left foot, executing five small striding steps. This should bring you back to your starting point with your right foot forward. As you finish moving, bring your bokken up into chudan.

As you move forward and back, you want to maintain strong focus and spirit. In other words, don't concentrate on moving so much that you lose focus on your partner. You should gaze at her with eyes slightly narrowed. When moving, your feet should slide forward and back as if you were wading through mud, giving a sense of stability and grounding.

OVERVIEW: THE FIRST FIVE KATA

Ipponme

This kata illustrates the effectiveness of a nuki technique. In it, both trainees assume jodan no kamae. They move forward to meet. Uchidachi takes the initiative and attacks with a men strike. Shidachi, demonstrating an awareness of the impending attack, steps back a half-step so that the attack misses, then steps in to deliver a men strike. Uchidachi steps back a half-step as if to try again, and shidachi lowers the point of the bokken to uchidachi's eyes. Uchidachi steps back another half-step and shidachi comes forward into left jodan, completely dominating the situation. Both Kendoka then step into chudan no kamae, lower their bokken into hodoku, and step back five paces into their original starting position.

Nihonme

In this kata, both Kendoka assume chudan no kamae. They step in to meet. Uchidachi cuts at shidachi's kote. Shidachi evades, in another example of nuki technique, by sliding diagonally to his left, lowering his bokken, and then cutting uchidachi's right kote. Shidachi then steps back into the center. Both assume chudan, lower their bokken to hodoku, and step back.

Sanbonme

This kata features the tsuki thrust. Both practitioners assume gedan no kamae, the low stance. They step in and raise swords slowly to chudan. Uchidachi steps forward right and attacks with a thrust to the throat. Shidachi takes a half-step back, and parries with the side of the bokken to his left. He then counters with three tsuki, stepping in right, left, and then right. Uchidachi steps back in response, parrying the first two thrusts. The final thrust is not parried. With his sword in uchidachi's face, shidachi takes three small steps forward, dominating uchidachi with the point of his sword. Shidachi then begins to step back. With the sword still dominating uchidachi, he takes two steps back (left, right). He then begins a series of three more steps, lowering his bokken to chudan. At the first step, uchidachi raises his bokken to meet shidachi at chudan, then steps forward on the next two steps. Both are now back in the center. They assume hodoku and step back five steps to the starting line.

Yohonme

At the starting point, uchidachi assumes right hasso no kamae. Shidachi assumes wakigamae. They take three steps forward. At this point, uchidachi slides forward, leading with his right foot, striking down with the bokken. Shidachi steps forward with his right foot, also striking down. Their swords clash high and are brought down into chudan. Uchidachi then attacks with a tsuki. Shidachi parries the thrust by turning his bokken on his side and pointing it to his right. At the same time, he slides diagonally to his left, then steps in to strike uchidachi's men. Shidachi then moves to the center, both assume chudan, then hodoku, and move back.

Gohonme

This kata utilizes the suriage technique to deflect and simultaneously attack. Uchidachi assumes left jodan no kamae. Shidachi assumes chudan. They step in. Shidachi raises his bokken slightly. Uchidachi attacks men. Shidachi slides his bokken upward, knocking the attack away and to his left, then cuts down to men. Shidachi then assumes left jodan and dominates the situation. Both Kendoka then assume chudan in center, then hodoku, then step back to the starting line.

A more detailed examination of the first five kata needed for advancement to the rank of shodan is presented on the following pages.

Ipponme

In this kata, the spirit is one of awareness and control. Each trainee moves in, poised to strike. Shidachi gains control of the situation by immediately responding to uchidachi's attack with nuki waza, moving slightly to evade the blow and countering decisively with one of his own.

This type of poise is extremely difficult to maintain, but it goes directly to the heart of Kendo training. Faced with a threat, an instinctive reaction is to evade that threat. In Kendo, however, we do not want to be slaves to our instinctive reactions, but rather to harness these reactions in the pursuit of something more sophisticated. In the situation presented in the first kata, merely evading an attack is not enough. To survive, we must respond offensively. A decisive counter will be the one that is the most efficient. In this case, we respond, not by denying our instinct to avoid, to get out of the way of the attack, but by harnessing and modifying that response. Here, the defender moves away, but only far enough to negate the efficacy of the attacker's strike. He then steps in decisively to counter with a focused attack of his own.

This response seems a simple one. It is, in fact, simple in its most profound sense—it is elegant, efficient—but try to put this into practice in your free sparring. You will soon see the value in practicing this kata over and over again as part of the process of unifying mind and body through the art of Kendo.

Technical considerations are as follows:

Both trainees assume jodan no kamae. Uchidachi begins the move into jodan first, followed almost immediately by shidachi. This pattern is repeated in all the kata, and indicates the aggressive nature of the attacker and the more pacific, responsive role of the defender. In making this move, uchidachi steps back with his right foot to assume a left jodan. Shidachi, standing in chudan, keeps his feet in place and raises his sword to jodan in response.

In jodan no kamae, the bokken is held above the head, pointing back and slightly to the right. The cutting edge faces the opponent. Trainees should be careful to hold the sword at a forty five degree angle to their rear, keeping the bokken from being held either too far back or too straight up. The hands should be placed above and slightly in front of the forehead.

Ipponme
(Part I)

1

2

3

4

Ipponme
(Part 2)

5

6

7

They move forward three steps to meet, uchidachi beginning with the left foot, shidachi with the right. They pause. Uchidachi takes the initiative and attacks with a men strike, giving the kiai "YAH!" He takes care to cut fully, slicing down below the horizontal and leaning slightly forward, demonstrating full commitment to the attack.

Shidachi, demonstrating an awareness of the impending attack, steps back a half-step with his left foot. He raises his hands slightly so that the attack misses, then steps in (right) to deliver a men strike, calling "TO!"

Uchidachi steps back a half-step (left) as if to try again, and shidachi lowers the point of the bokken to uchidachi's eyes. Uchidachi steps back another half-step (left), and shidachi comes forward into left jodan, completely dominating the situation.

Both Kendoka then step into chudan no kamae (shidachi bringing the leading left foot back behind him), maintaining a strong focus, lower their bokken into hodoku, and step back five paces (alternating left-right) into their original starting position of chudan no kamae.

8

9

Nihonme

This kata is another example of nuki waza. Here, the defender eludes an attack to the kote and retaliates in kind, utilizing distance and timing to defeat the opponent.

The action in the second kata seems a bit more "natural" to the novice than that of the first kata. Here, we dodge and attack by moving out of the way and placing ourselves in a good position to counter. It has none of the reversal of momentum that makes the technique in the first kata so hard to replicate in sparring. Its value lies in the demonstration that a good Kendoka has to think of distance and position as having more dimensions than in a simple linear model. As we struggle to master the techniques of Kendo, our focus is so strongly placed on the waza at hand that we tend to move mechanically and predictably in a straight line forward and back. Yet free sparring is just that—free. There are many directions to move in, and we need to begin to experiment with different patterns of movement and their implications for our technique. Through practicing the second kata, we come to the realization that, by moving to the side, we can subtly change the dynamics of an encounter to our advantage.

In this kata, both Kendoka assume chudan no kamae. They step in to meet, using the standard three-step pattern. Both are in right chudan no kamae.

Uchidachi cuts at shidachi's kote, "YAH!"

Shidachi evades, in another example of nuki technique, by sliding diagonally in to his left rear. At the same time, he lowers his bokken.

The action deprives uchidachi of his target. Having evaded, shidachi raises his sword, and, shuffling forward slightly, cuts uchidachi's right kote, "TO!"

Making a strong chudan, shidachi then steps back into the center, leading with his right foot. Since he has dominated the situation, it is uchidachi's role to respond to this move by lowering his sword in such a way as to permit shidachi to move to the center without interference. Uchidachi follows shidachi's lead and assumes chudan no kamae.

From chudan, both lower their bokken to hodoku, and step back five small paces to assume chudan at the starting point.

Sanbonme

This kata features the tsuki thrust and parries against it.

If the first two kata seem to cast shidachi in a somewhat reactive role, the third kata demonstrates the importance of an aggressive spirit in responding to attack. Here, shidachi successfully parries a tsuki attack and immediately goes on the offensive in the same manner, driving his opponent back. Shidachi uses a series of thrusts to unsettle his attacker and, demonstrating the utility of multiple attacks, uses repeated tsuki waza to gain ascendancy over uchidachi. The extensive use of tsuki waza in this kata gives it an aggressive, dangerous feel. The two performers are also moving a great deal more than in the previous two kata, making this a dynamic kata that stresses each Kendoka's ability to maintain balance and proper technique in the face of a dangerous thrusting attack with a hardwood sword.

From the beginning position, both practitioners assume gedan no kamae, the low stance. In gedan, the sword is held in the center of the body, with the tip lowered to about knee height. As you assume gedan, be careful not to let your gaze follow the point of the sword. You should maintain focus on your opponent.

The swordsmen step in three steps and raise swords slowly to chudan. Uchidachi steps forward right and attacks with a thrust to the solar plexus, "YAH!" sliding the side of his sword (the *shinogi*) against that of his opponent. As he thrusts, he turns the sword sideways, cutting edge facing to his right.

Shidachi takes a half-step back with the left foot and parries with the side of the bokken to his left. The parry is effected by bringing the hilt of his sword slightly to his left side, turning the blade so that the cutting edge faces to the right.

Sanbonme (Part 1)

Sanbonme (Part 2)

Shidachi then counters with two tsuki, stepping in right, "TO!" and then left. In these thrusts, the sword is not turned to the side. Uchidachi steps back in response (right, then left), parrying the two thrusts by bringing the tip of the sword under and around the tip of shidachi's weapon and attempting to come into chudan.

What seems like three further thrusts are actually a technique known as seme—an aggressive advance where, if the uchidachi did not retreat, shidachi would essentially impale uchidachi on the bokken as he advanced. Shidachi focuses his sword and steps three times (right, left, right), raising the sword to uchidachi's eye level and completely dominating the situation. When stepping in, shidachi should drive from the hips, gaining momentum with each step, so that the second and third steps in are taken in an increasingly accelerated manner.

Uchidachi steps back (left, right, left) in response to this *seme*, lowering his sword to gedan.

Shidachi then begins to step back. With the sword still dominating uchidachi, he takes two steps back (left, right), lowering his sword to chudan. At the first step, uchidachi offers no response. At shidachi's second step, uchidachi raises his sword to meet shidachi's in chudan.

Shidachi now steps back three more times (left, right, left), finishing in chudan. Uchidachi mirrors this movement by stepping forward (right, left, right). Care should be taken that the bokken stay crossed as this movement is performed.

Both are now back in the center. They assume hodoku and step back five steps to the starting line.

Yohonme

This kata demonstrates the technique of parrying and using the position of the parry to launch a response. In the kata, this parry is much more pronounced than it would be in a match using shinai. In a sparring situation, this technique would be a type of kaeshi waza.

With an increasing mastery of the basics of Kendo comes an appreciation of the more subtle dimensions to the art. Some of these have to do with the tension, play, and responses that can be created by the crossing of swords (or shinai). It is said that masters of the art can tell a great deal about a swordsman merely by the feel of crossing swords with him. This points out the fact that the contact we make with our weapons can have an impact on the success of our encounters. The fourth kata is an introduction to the role that more subtle sliding and deflecting motions can have in negating attacks and providing us with an opportunity to respond effectively.

At the starting point, uchidachi steps forward with the left foot and assumes right hasso no kamae.

Hasso is a traditional stance not very frequently used in Kendo, but we preserve it here. In hasso, you raise the sword up and bring it to your right side. The tsuba should be at about the same level as your mouth. The point of the sword angles back slightly.

In response to this motion, shidachi assumes wakigamae. He brings the right foot back behind the left, lowers the tip of the sword to the rear, hands held to the right side at hip level. The original intent of this stance was to make it difficult for the opponent to gauge the length of your weapon (before the standardization of modern times, swords were of varying lengths).

Yohonme (Part 1)

Both take three steps forward, each beginning with the left foot.

At this point, uchidachi slides forward, leading with his right foot, striking in a broad slashing motion down at the men. Shidachi steps forward with his right foot, also striking down at the same target. Their swords clash high and are brought down into chudan. The sense here is that both swordsmen have attempted the same attack and are forestalled.

Be careful here not to attempt to hit each other's sword: this will cause your men strikes to deteriorate. Instead of cutting straight down as they should, the strikes will slant in toward the other's sword. The point here is not to smash the opponent's sword aside, but to have the simultaneous actions of the two men cuts negate each other.

Yohonme (Part 2)

5

6

7

Uchidachi then attacks with a tsuki, "YAH!," sword turned with the cutting edge to the right. Shidachi parries the thrust by turning his bokken on his side and pointing it to his right. This permits him to control the attacker's thrust and allows it to be redirected to slide harmlessly past shidachi.

Simultaneously, shidachi slides diagonally to his left and brings the right foot to the rear position, then steps in left to strike uchidachi's men, "TO!"

At the completion of this attack, Shidachi then moves to the center, uchidachi retracting his sword as both assume chudan, then hodoku, and move back five steps to their original positions.

Gohonme

This kata utilizes the suriage technique to deflect and simultaneously attack. Its footwork is very similar to that of the first kata, but is uses a much more sophisticated method of negating the strike.

Uchidachi assumes left jodan no kamae. Shidachi assumes chudan. Shidachi then raises his bokken slightly in response to uchidachi's threatening jodan position. They step in, uchidachi beginning with the left foot, shidachi with the right.

Uchidachi attacks men, "YAH!" by stepping in with his right foot.

Gohonme (Part 1)

Gohonme (Part 2)

Shidachi steps back with his left foot, in much the same way as in the first kata. Here, however, he does not rely on footwork alone to negate uchidachi's attack. Shidachi turns his sword slightly so that the cutting edge faces to the left (protecting his right hand). Simultaneously, he raises his sword up in preparation for an attack. The rising action of the bokken acts to deflect uchidachi's attack up and to shidachi's left.

As the cut is deflected, shidachi steps in and cuts down to men. He then steps back with his right foot, assumes the left jodan position, and dominates the situation.

Shidachi then retracts his left foot and assumes chudan; uchidachi steps forward in response and adopts the same posture. Uchidachi then takes three small steps back, beginning with the left foot. Shidachi responds by taking three small steps forward, beginning with the right foot.

Both Kendoka then assume chudan in center, then hodoku, then step back five steps to the starting line.

PERFORMANCE DYNAMICS

Kata are a form of abstract, symbolic, or heavily significant performance. As we have discussed, they are a way to enshrine and pass on certain key lessons learned by swordsmen in Kendo's past. On a certain level, therefore, they are about skill: its demonstration and its perpetuation.

Gohonme (Part 3)

Kata are also about poise and self-presentation. One of the rationales behind training with the wooden sword is to take away the protective shield of bogu and have Kendoka engage in the reenactment of decisive moments in swordplay. By using more dangerous weapons and abandoning our armor, we subject ourselves to a different type of experience and a different type of scrutiny than when sparring. Even though kata are set patterns, the fact that they are performed with and in reaction to another human being makes subtle demands on the individual. Not only are questions of timing and distance brought into play, so too are questions of mental poise and balance as you work your way through the kata.

This means that, for a kata performance to be truly admirable, both uchidachi and shidachi must have a solid grasp of their roles in the action. A flaw in our understanding of a particular kata is immediately apparent to an examining judge: the hesitation, the slight stammer in our technique, a momentary loss of balance, are all indicators that the Kendoka has not mastered the kata.

With this in mind, trainees should practice kata regularly (not just immediately prior to a promotion shiai), taking care to master the movements and their sequence as both uchidachi and shidachi. This is particularly important since, prior to an examination, you have no way of knowing which role you will be required to take.

Once the sequence of action has been grasped, the trainee also needs to reflect on the lesson being imparted and the dynamics of the actions embodied in the particular kata. You need to be able to immerse yourself in the role you are playing and to invest your actions with intensity and meaning. Only then will your kata performance begin to reflect how well you are beginning to grasp some of Kendo's most important lessons.

V O I D

The ideas suggested by the term "Void" were significant to Musashi and other martial artists like him. The concept was strongly influenced by centuries of thought and reflection in traditions as varied as Confucianism, Daoism, Shinto, and Buddhism. When Musashi uses "Void," he is referring to what he considered to be the most profound, underlying concept of swordsmanship and, indeed, of the universe. Void, he felt, served as the underpinning of the martial (and all other) arts. Musashi felt, as type of fundamental principle, that the spiritual insight gained through seeking to understand the Void gave the swordsman's quest a type of transcendent meaning.

Despite this conviction, the Void section of *Go Rin No Sho* is the briefest of the book. Yet the implications of Musashi's stress on a transcendent purpose to the martial way suggest that the subject is well worth our consideration. Musashi's short entry does not reflect a sense that this is a topic that can be neglected by the martial artist. It may be, however, that he felt that some things need to be experienced and cannot be truly described in print.

I tend to agree with Musashi on this point. Nonetheless, it is important that a book on Kendo include some discussion of its more profound dimensions. This is all the more important because Kendo is a very human activity to which practitioners bring all their frailties, which sometimes makes it easy to lose sight of Kendo's true purpose.

Like any activity (including any martial art), Kendo can be understood on a number of different levels. Certainly a large part of this book has focused on the more technical aspects. Human beings, however, have an intriguing propensity to invest activities with implications and meanings that transcend immediate utility. Kendo is certainly a physical exercise in its most basic sense. It is also a competitive sport, with all the excitement that engenders. Of course, in addition, Kendo is a "martial art." As such, it has its origins in combat techniques developed by Japan's feudal warriors. Yet, as we have seen, Kendo's techniques have in reality evolved into a body of idealized abstractions that have little or nothing to do with practical questions of self-defense. Kendo, it is true, can improve our stamina and our reflexes and also help us attain a type of calm focus in hectic situations. These are, of course, qualities that are of use to martial artists in general. But if a trainee is seeking "street applications," he or she had best look elsewhere.

Finally, we need to admit that there is a psychological dimension to the practice of this art, and this may be the most significant aspect of Kendo. The mental engagement Kendo demands reveals it as a vastly complex type of activity, which ultimately enmeshes both the body and mind in a unified type of action. In this regard, Kendo training is a type of "flow" experience as described by some modern psychologists.

Even at this most cursory level, then, it is easy to see how multidimensional Kendo's significance is.

At its core, the art is more than just another pasttime, sport, or form of exercise. Kendo is a Way. The very name of this art begs the question, however: "a way to what?"

The philosophical and spiritual aspects of the modern Japanese martial arts are recognized in theory by many people. For a large number of martial artists, this spiritual dimension is a major factor in attracting them to the arts in the first place. In Kendo, it is not unusual to find out that many trainees have come to swordsmanship via other arts: their journey along the martial way has been a long one and, as they progress, they are constantly seeking richer dimensions to their training.

Of course, trainees have been attempting to explore the richness of the martial arts for centuries. For many modern Kendoka, who have been raised outside the Japanese or East Asian cultural traditions, the question is not whether this is important, but rather how we can most clearly attempt a similar exploration.

I would suggest that we use the very concrete experience of training as discussed in earlier chapters to give us a clue. When we look at the characteristics of Kendo practice, we find that there are at least three significant emphases that stand out. The first is an emphasis on decorum, dignity, and a unique type of presence that is required of Kendoka. The second is an insistence on adherence to a particular code of behavior. The third, and most subtle, is a suggestion, through various symbolic means, that what we are about in training is something transcendent and not strictly utilitarian in a martial sense.

Look, for instance, at the training uniform of Kendo. The hakama is easily one of the most elaborate pieces of martial arts finery commonly employed. It is also possessed of an esthetic quality that lends grace to action within the Kendo dojo. Why this insistence on the hakama as part of the uniform of Kendo? It is certainly possible to practice the art in almost any type of clothing. The practitioners of *jukendo*, a martial arts form based on bayonet fighting, wear armor similar to Kendo's and yet wear a karate-like uniform. The clothes worn for Kendo, then, are not practical. They are nonetheless important for other reasons.

The hakama is part of a uniform meant to impart a certain dignity to the wearer. It is meant to symbolize a connection to centuries of tradition and to invest the trainee with the refinement and sense of importance that go with significant human endeavors.

For Kendo is an approach to self-cultivation. In this sense, it is part of a larger philosophy in East Asia that stresses the merit in self-improvement. Certainly in the Confucian tradition (which originated in China but had a strong effect on Japan and Korea as well), the idea that people would benefit from the refinement that was created by the act of studying, training, and working to improve themselves was an important concept. Confucian thinkers tended to stress the inherent ability of people to better themselves and, by virtue of that effort, to have a positive effect on their world. The demanding training of Confucian scholars, which stressed a mastery of basic skills such as calligraphy and a fidelity to the form and principles embodied in a collection of "classic" literary works, was echoed in approaches to other endeavors. The martial arts were one category of such endeavors.

The feudal Japanese, with a dominant class of warriors, developed a tradition that, in part, emphasized the potential that martial training had for human development. They came to believe that the high standards and fidelity to form and principle found in martial training were not, in a spiritual sense, different from those embodied in more scholarly and "refined" activities. Hence the widely known saying *bun bu ichi*—the way of the pen and the way of the sword are the same.

The training methods and emphases in martial arts instruction, then, are consciously maintained as part of a body of technique that relates to the inner development of the individual. This is an important point. Beginners in various martial arts, Kendo included, are often attracted by witnessing the seemingly effortless grace of masters. But the process of achieving mastery is long, repetitive, and possessed of a rigid insistence that we adhere to custom, etiquette, and (as it sometimes feels) an archaic, inefficient approach to teaching physical skills.

The masters would say that this estimation is both true and false. Training in Kendo is rigid. But it appears inefficient only to those who fail to understand that training in the art is about both the sword and the spirit.

We have seen throughout the text that there is a prescribed way to do almost everything in Kendo—from putting on your uniform to entering and leaving the room to folding your hakama—and this insistence that trainees partake in Kendo's tradition is a reflection of the conviction that learning the proper way to manage yourself and relate to your surroundings is the mark of a refined individual.

Technically, Kendo is an art of precision, and its techniques are judged by an absolute standard. This quality, too, speaks of a particular mind-set.

Like the Confucians, Kendo sensei believe that there are absolute standards of excellence we can measure ourselves against. This is a decidedly traditional type of world-view. Although many in the modern world feel that value judgments are inherently unfair or wrong, Kendo's world view is one that is very sure of itself. As a result, it is not enough for a Kendoka to be effective in sparring. This "take what is useful" approach, so popular with other martial artists (particularly American ones), is out of place in a Kendo dojo. For Kendo sensei, functionality is a direct result of adherence to form.

The spirit of the move is important, not necessarily its outcome. This is because such an approach stresses the inner state of the trainee. From this perspective, the effort involved in attempting to meet an exacting standard and the sincerity with which we pursue that standard are what is vital. Ideally, good form and effective technique should go together. If one has to be sacrificed, however, Kendo sensei will opt to see effectiveness go. After all, if we are training to develop ourselves, it makes little difference how our actions fare in a contest. Thus, success in sparring is not a prerequisite for promotion into the lower dan ranks: you can be judged proficient in Kendo simply upon the mastery of basic skills and a demonstration of the character needed for this.

At the same time that Kendo turns relentlessly inward, it must be admitted that, as an art founded on the incidence of conflict in a duel, it also attempts to develop the individual character by turning outward through contest.

The psychological aspects of human competition are well known. In Kendo, the excitement of a match is a type of laboratory used to test a Kendoka's development. Trainees often focus on formal tournament or promotion bouts as occasions that evaluate progress. The truth of the matter is that every time two Kendoka cross shinai, they are being tested and evaluated. The test, of course, is to see how well they have acquired both Kendo's technique and its mind-set. The techniques, as we have seen, must adhere to formal standards. The mind-set is expressed in part through good spirit, a strong shout, and proper focus and zanshin. And yet a more severe test of the spirit is how the individual reacts to occasions of victory and defeat—letting neither the elation of winning nor the disappointment of losing sway the trainee from a sincere pursuit of self perfection.

In terms of individual character development, it may be that the masters stress contests so much for reasons that are very different from what you might expect.

Of course they value strong demonstrations of spirit and good Kendo technique—this serves as an example to others and a validation of everything trainees strive for. Yet it may be that they also value contests for the temptations they provide—temptations involving pride, or depression, anger, or fear—and the ways in which these temptations challenge students to rise above them.

A second theme in Kendo is the concept that discipleship in this art involves a type of subordination to a larger order in order to accomplish greater ends. To train in Kendo is also to be enmeshed in a community of learners. This implies something about Kendo's ideas regarding how people relate to one another and the rights and obligations each of us has in relation to wider society.

The Japanese word for training is keiko, which literally means to reflect on things from the past. In Kendo, part of what we do when we train is to honor those masters who have gone before us. We do this through emulating the techniques and kata that have been developed and by doing our best to pass them accurately on to others. This type of orientation implies something very important. It communicates the fact that, for Kendoka, the experience of other human beings is important. What has been learned in the past is worthy of learning again today, since this will create a solid base for further advancement. We are also charged with passing these lessons on to others as part of the responsibility we have to the larger community.

In this sense, the pursuit of the Way of the Sword is not a purely introspective or selfish act. We engage in training not for our own development alone but also because to do so forges another link in a long chain of learners that spans the centuries.

In other words, with privilege comes responsibility.

This idea is one that also springs from Confucian ideology and the historical experience of the samurai. The ancestral forms of swordsmanship that led to Kendo were developed by the feudal warriors of Japan. A translation of the word samurai is "those who serve," and this provides a good point from which to begin the discussion of this aspect of Kendo.

The "superior man" of Confucianism was expected to take an active and positive role in larger society. In fact, for over one thousand years, government functionaries in China's various dynastic empires were selected from among the most able scholars in the land.

The samurai of Japan also played an active part in the society of their day. They were intimately involved in the struggles and politics of feudal Japan and, as "those who serve," they were obligated to do so. There were benefits to such expectations, of course—as a ruling elite the samurai helped make and enforce the law and enjoyed a wide variety of privileges. There were also drawbacks—it was the samurai who fought and were expected to die for their political rulers. The widely known custom of ritual suicide (seppuku) was an expression of how deeply committed a samurai warrior was expected to be to his lord and his cause.

In a larger sense, this involvement of the samurai with wider society led to the development of an idea that with the enhanced power and accomplishment of the trained warrior came some fairly serious obligations. This was, in part, the impetus for the development of a theory of behavior known as bushido. Part political and legal guidebook, part philosophical manifesto, the body of work written around the topic over the years served to link the idea of social service with martial prowess.

The development of an ideological component to martial training has been going on in Japan for at least five-hundred years. Warriors and philosophers thought about the role of the fighter in society and approached it from a number of perspectives. This has led to a very complex and multi-faceted "philosophy" for the Japanese martial arts. Depending on the individual tradition or style or teacher, different aspects of this ideological heritage are emphasized. Kendo, which is a modern distillation and reinterpretation of the martial technique and theory surrounding swordsmanship, has been shaped by a variety of influences. Some (but not all) significant ones are discussed here.

The Yagyu family of swordsmen—who became the official fencing instructors of the Tokugawa shoguns—were but one example of excellent swordsmen who also came to understand something of how individual achievement in the martial arts needed to be linked to an awareness of social obligations. Yagyu Munenori, for instance, is one of the most famous of the Yagyu swordsmen because of his exploration of the relationship between Zen Buddhism and the warrior's calling. His interest was sparked both by a concern for the relationship between training and personal development, and by a need to understand how the martial artist should behave in larger society. In this, he was influenced by his father, Muneyoshi, who was also an accomplished swordsman in his own right and an individual who had strong ideas about how a warrior was to conduct himself in life.

These men lived during the sixteenth and seventeenth centuries. In the 1500s, the stage was set in Japan for a series of conflicts that would pit feudal lords and their retainers against each other. The prize was domination of Japan. In a time of war, samurai had the opportunity to extensively test their skills on the battlefield. As the century drew to a close and Japan was united under the rule of the Tokugawa family, however, warriors were presented with a new challenge—how could they best serve their masters in a new, more peaceful era?

For the Yagyu family, this led to a realization that swordsmanship was not just about combat. That fighting skills were an important part of a samurai's identity was undeniable. Yet the Yagyu came to believe that the warrior's training and perspective could be useful in other ways as well.

Munenori came to believe that righteousness is an essential part of the martial arts. Without this moral dimension, swordsmanship is merely the act of killing and avoiding being killed. Munenori therefore came to think that swordsmanship should make a more positive contribution to human society by creating individuals who were disciplined, steadfast, and focused.

He wrote the *Heiho Kadensho*, or *Chronicles of Strategy*, to record his insights for future swordsmen. Like other scrolls from the traditional martial ryu of Japan, this work is difficult to understand on a technical level. It nonetheless is an example of the evolving complex of ideas that surrounded martial training.

Munenori's most enduring contribution to the practice of the Japanese sword arts, however, is his stress on Zen concepts as a route to mastery and his insistence that true swordsmanship is a moral art. The influence of Yagyu thought on the practice of sword arts is the conviction that training should in some way be directed toward serving a higher goal than mere technical perfection. In other words, the skill acquired should be used for objectives other than mere personal glory.

These ideas were shared by other masters as well. Odagiri Sekiei, founder of the Muji-Shin-Jen Ryu of swordsmanship, also thought of it not as an art of killing but of disciplining the self as a moral being. His "Sword of No-Abiding Mind" style encouraged a type of technical and spiritual development that would lead to a mastery of the sword so complete that it would be unnecessary for the swordsman to slay his opponent. We can see that the influence of this sort of perspective has affected the practice of modern budo quite strongly. This perspective is perhaps most strongly echoed in the theoretical underpinnings of the aikido of Ueshiba Morihei, who had extensive exposure to classical weapons systems.

Kendo, too, has inherited this ideological tradition: Kendo views train-ing as a way of creating socially responsible individuals. For the Japanese, the act of disciplining oneself to a particular system or style of doing things—whether it is calligraphy, or flower arrangement, or the martial arts—is an implicit acceptance of a type of social order and a signal of the willingness of an individual to live by its values and rules. In this sense, the discipline inherent in Kendo is meant to mirror the demands society as a whole makes upon each of us.

Kendo stresses hierarchy. This is an important concept in Japanese society, where relative positions of inferior and superior status serve as a guide to proper behavior. In Kendo, we achieve our status by virtue of our accomplishment in the art. In other words, we define ourselves through a common body of rules and requirements that lead to rank classifications in terms of kyu and dan, students and sensei. We define ourselves in rela-tion to others. As our accomplishment in Kendo advances, what is required of us changes. In a very familiar sort of pattern, the greater your accomplishment, the greater the expectations others have of you.

These expectations are not just technical ones, for "spirit" is highly val-ued in Kendo. Spirit is an outward manifestation of our inward state—in other words, it is how we express our true grasp of Kendo. The spirit with which we approach difficult training and the way in which we interact with other trainees are of utmost concern.

This is why Kendo's etiquette is so well developed. It is not just that the various forms of politeness make for a better training environment—bowing when ready to engage in keiko helps us to avoid all sorts of unpleasant accidents—they also serve to reinforce basic principles of human interaction.

In Kendo, the bow is a signal of respect. We bow on entering and leaving the practice hall. We bow to the kamiza as a sign of our reverence for the art and its traditions. But we also bow to each other.

"Do"

Bowing to a senior is a sign of respect and, in a way, submission to his or her guidance. But seniors bow to lower ranks as well. This is an acknowledgment of the basic respect and civility due to all people. It is also a sign that the senior honors the effort and intent of the trainee. It is, in short, an acknowledgment of the importance of any human being and, in the context of Kendo training, an acknowledgment that walking along this martial path is an endeavor worthy of respect, no matter what the level of accomplishment.

It is hoped that this attitude of respect and mutual consideration will infuse all dealings Kendoka have with others, both in the dojo and out. Part of the impact of following a Way is to have its basic precepts infuse our daily life. In its stress on the dignity of each individual and the worth of endeavors linked to commonly held values, the lessons learned through Kendo have great potential to enhance our lives in this way.

The third theme in Kendo is one that, through various symbolic mechanisms, sends the message that, while we are engaged in training in this art, we are also engaged in something more important than just fighting.

A symbol is usually something that has more significance than its outward appearance would suggest. I have already discussed the growing abstraction of swordsmanship that has evolved in Kendo—the way weapons and armor and rules of engagement have been codified into a more abstract form of fighting. I would now like to take this discussion one step further.

Look at the shinai, the preeminent implement used in Kendo training. It is an elegant and functional tool, a conglomeration of bamboo and leather. In training, it stands for the sword. But we know that its shape and dynamics really have little in common with the katana. This is one of the reasons that we also use bokken in training—to retain some more realistic contact with what it would be like to use a real sword. Yet the shinai is important because it is an integral part of how we learn Kendo.

We know that the shinai was developed late in the sixteenth century, eventually evolving into its modern form as a way of making training safer. Yet the continuing development of abstraction in Kendo's equipment and techniques take this process to a point where, as I have maintained, Kendo is no longer a truly "martial" type of endeavor.

This was done quite purposefully. And at least part of the rationale for doing this is to remind Kendoka, even as they swirl in heated mock combat, that all this effort and focus are really about something other than fighting. This is a central tenet of modern Kendo's philosophy.

Kendo's roots stretch back to the time when swordsmanship was a true fighting system. Even then, however, there were masters who were fearsome fighters and yet believers that there was an "added dimension" to martial training. This added dimension was one that was thought to have both mental and spiritual aspects, although different masters typically emphasized one aspect or the other.

Kagehisa Ittosai Ito, for instance, has had a strong influence on the development of Kendo. While not one who laid stress on the spiritual dimensions of swordsmanship, he was a champion of the idea that there was a mental component to mastery. For Ittosai, composure was a critical mental element in mastering the sword.

He perceived an underlying unity in sword techniques that echoes in a way Musashi's concept of Void—a fundamental principle that reflected the cosmic order. Ittosai believed that all sword techniques come from one single technique, that of *kiriotoshi*.

For Ittosai, this meant that the route to mastery was essentially one of training in the basics. This, in turn, could also lead to a comprehension of the true nature of reality. His conviction in the validity of his philosophy—one Mind, one Sword, one Technique—was reflected in his adoption of the name Ittosai, which means "One Sword Man." A strong stress on basic techniques and the importance of mental focus was perpetuated in the Itto Ryu he founded in the sixteenth century. So compelling were his insights that they continued to inspire disciples for generations. Certainly, this emphasis on a fidelity to form and the perfection of basic technique, all contained within a system stressing the mental dimensions of swordsmanship, has strongly influenced the development of modern Kendo.

Of course, Miyamoto Musashi is perhaps the most renowned swordsman of this period, and was another significant thinker in martial arts philosophy.

Musashi founded the Niten Ichi Ryu and, like others, was deeply interested in the impact that mental training had on technique. While not overtly spiritual, he was, nonetheless, influenced by the Zen concept of no-mind. Musashi expressed this concept with the term Void and identified true attainment of the way of swordsmanship with the attainment of Void. We see here a common theme echoed in the thoughts of various masters. In this state, the swordsman becomes a stable, focused, imperturbable entity; in Musashi's words, he attains the "body of a rock" in which he is able to go beyond merely seeing the opponent and can perceive his strengths and weaknesses and even anticipate his actions. The concept of the distinction between perception and sight in swordplay is one that has endured to this day and is a concern of advanced Kendoka.

Kamiizumi Nobutsuna, another sixteenth-century kenshi, was trained in the tradition of the Kage (Shadow) Ryu, but made a number of changes that prompted him to change his system's name to Shin-Kage (New Shadow). His emphasis on the mind and mental control in the practice of swordsmanship was very influential.

In this regard, we once again witness the influence of the Yagyu. Yagyu Muneyoshi was deeply impressed by his study of Shin-Kage. His son Munenori was stylistically guided by the precepts of Shin-Kage, and, as a result of its concern with the mind, was also led to a more focused exploration of the impact that Zen Buddhism could have on swordsmen. He developed a lifelong friendship with the Zen monk Takuan, who wrote the famous philosophical treatise the *Fudo Shinmyo Roku* as a way of helping Munenori explore the relationship between the sword and the mind.

Munenori was interested, like Ittosai and Nobutsuna, in the relation between mental states and swordsmanship. He consequently became fascinated by Zen Buddhism and its emphasis on clearing the mind of distractions and coming to a true perception of the universe. Takuan taught that a mind unclouded by illusion would be able to react instantaneously to any attack. In this very practical sense, Munenori thought that training in Zen's meditative techniques would be useful.

His thinking about the sword was a bit more complex than that, however. Munenori became increasingly convinced that his style of swordsmanship had nothing at all to do with swordsmanship, and everything to do with the spirit. He even remarked that if his style of swordplay had not already been titled the Yagyu Shinkage Ryu by his father, he would call it the *Muto*, or No-Sword, Ryu, to underscore this fact.

As a result of his convictions regarding the social role of the warrior and the impact of Zen on his outlook, Munenori believed that swordsmen must aspire to a plane beyond life and death, must cast off petty distractions if they are to achieve real mastery. In this way, spiritual development and martial prowess became insolubly linked.

This ideological current had been flowing throughout many different martial systems in feudal Japan. It was often said, for instance, that true swordsmanship was not a matter of just technique, but of the development of a comprehensive mental and philosophical stance often labeled as "heiho," or strategy. The Yagyu family certainly included this in their reflections on the way of the sword. The philosophical inspirations for this trend were varied, and included Shinto, Confucianism, and Buddhism. Munenori's interpretation was relatively unique because of his strong engagement with Zen.

The growing impact of Zen on the thinking of martial artists is exemplified by Yamaoka Tesshu (1836–1888), whose life and career spanned the interval during which Japan entered the modern world and also the period in which swordsmanship ceased to be a real military art and evolved into a true form of budo.

Tesshu was a complex man: an accomplished calligrapher, a serious student of Zen, an active public figure (serving both the Tokugawa shogunate and the new government of the Emperor Meiji), and a master swordsman.

Martial arts study was a major theme in his life. Tesshu studied in the Shinkage Ryu, Ono-ha Itto Ryu, and Nakanishi-ha Itto Ryu, becoming one of the foremost swordsmen of the era. Although he was deeply committed to Zen, it should not be thought that Tesshu was a less than vigorous martial artist: he stood over six feet tall, was immensely strong, and his swordplay was so enthusiastic that he was nicknamed "Demon Tetsu." In fact, in some dojo he was forbidden from striking the kote area for fear that he would break his partner's arms!

What marked Tesshu as a great swordsman, however, was not his physical expertise, but the emphasis he eventually placed on the disciplining of the mind and spirit.

He came to this perspective gradually, by virtue of his own experience. When he was twenty-eight, at the height of his strength, Tesshu was decisively defeated by Asari Gimei, master swordsman of the Nakanishi-ha Itto Ryu, who was not only twelve years older than Tesshu, but about half his size. To a fencer used to dominating his opponents by virtue of both his skill and size, such a defeat was practically inconceivable. Yet Asari was so powerful a kenshi that Tesshu found all mental composure fleeing the moment he crossed swords with the master. Tesshu, a vigorous young fencer with powerful technique, came to realize that he was defeated, not by physical prowess, but by the spiritual force of Asari.

This was clearly an important turning point for Tesshu, and his experience influenced his approach to swordsmanship. He became Asari's disciple and also intensified his study of Zen. After seventeen years in both Asari's and a Zen dojo, at age forty-five, Tesshu experienced a type of

enlightenment, a psychospiritual revelation of sudden and striking importance. The poem he wrote about the experience clearly illustrates his
conviction that the way of the sword eventually leads to spiritual ends:

For years I forged my spirit through the study of swordsmanship,
confronting every challenge steadfastly.
The walls surrounding me suddenly crumbled;
like pure dew reflecting the world in crystal clarity, total
Awakening has now come.

With Tesshu's spiritual awakening, he truly gained mastery of the sword.
Asari designated him headmaster of his ryu and, it is said, never picked
up a sword again.

In the relationship between Zen and swordsmanship, we see the development of perhaps the most mature philosophical system in budo. At the
same time, we need to be cautious. There is a certain link between Zen
Buddhism and the martial arts in general. It is true that Zen has had a
powerful impact on individuals such as Munenori and Tesshu, and on
some of the modern martial ways, but much of this influence is relatively
recent, and has only developed during the twentieth century. While some
of this emphasis in Kendo is certainly a result of long historical development, related to the swordsmen discussed, some is not.

At least part of Zen's modern influence on the martial arts has to do
with an effort to emphasize the more peaceful aspects of the martial arts
after the Second World War.

It has been assumed that Zen influenced the outlook of Japanese warriors during the Kamakura and later eras, although evidence from the primary documents of the martial arts during this period seems to be lacking.

We know that Zen influenced some master swordsmen. It has to be admitted, however, that the central spiritual trend in martial training, at least until the Tokugawa era (1600–1868), was not a search for enlightenment, but rather a search for supernatural techniques to enhance combat performance. It is interesting to note, for instance, that the majority of inscriptions engraved on the tang of medieval Japanese swords were inspired by the canons of Esoteric, not Zen, Buddhism.

It is debatable whether or not the similarities between Zen and the martial arts are the result of the fact that Buddhism shaped budo throughout Japanese history. The most we can say is that more modern interpretations have given the philosophy of Zen a greater role to play than in centuries past. The fact that this is a relatively recent phenomenon, however, doesn't mean that it isn't significant. Kendo, after all, is a relatively recent phenomenon itself.

Once you escape from the debate on whether Zen shaped budo or vice versa, the question becomes why it has been possible to create such a strong relationship between what seem like two very different things.

The question of influence aside, I believe that it can be stressed that Kendo and Zen share similar outlooks and training techniques for two reasons. One is because they both developed in the same cultural environment. The other, more important reason, is that Kendo and Zen are ultimately striving toward similar goals: the liberation of the human spirit.

When we look at Kendo and Zen, we first find a common emphasis on technique as a means for achieving certain ends. The process of discipleship in both traditions is an austere one. Training in both disciplines is relentless, and is often composed of regimented, monotonous actions designed to challenge students' physical and mental states of mind.

The simple repetition of techniques in the Kendo dojo, for example, is thought to be the vehicle that will bring one to mastery. There is little explanation of significance, or even detailed analysis of the mechanics of a technique. By concentrating totally on the action, by countless repetitions, it is thought that the trainee will lose himself in movement. This will make the action a "natural" one, and gives it the speed and focus that are absent as long as the trainee maintains the distinction between thinking and doing, between himself and the art. Here we see the heritage of Ittosai.

The training exercises we use today such as kirikaeshi, suburi, and uchikomi, may thus be understood as forms of discipline used to promote focus and clarity, and are part of a central lesson concerning the total engagement in the here and now required of the Kendoka.

These actions, as well as kata, can in many ways be seen as the moving version of zazen (meditation), so central to Zen Buddhism. The Yagyu swordsmen, we recall, also felt that there was an important advantage conferred on a swordsman through the practice of Zen techniques. In Kendo, the difficulty involved in performing waza correctly time after time, and of letting no stray thoughts intrude to break the concentration is analogous to the experience of meditation. Here, the individual attempts to quiet the mind, to let thoughts come and go as they please until they bubble off, leaving the mind clear. In this way, followers of Zen believe, they will come to a "true" perception of reality.

The close link in the Japanese mind between zazen and techniques such as suburi was most clearly stressed by Yamaoka Tesshu. He was convinced, from his personal experience of Zen enlightenment, that training in the way of the sword was an intensely spiritual thing. In his dojo, known as the Shumpukan, Tesshu designed a training program calculated to exhaust the swordsman physically, and to develop an extremely clear and focused mind.

To stress the link between sword and spirit, Tesshu established his own ryu, the Muto (No-Sword) Ryu. Here we see a continuation of the idea that so inspired Yagyu Munenori.

Now the interesting thing was that, at Tesshu's school, despite his deep philosophical convictions, there was little or no emphasis on explanation or analysis of technique. Novice swordsmen devoted their time to repetitive forms of attack practice for at least three years. Tesshu thought that such training served to both strengthen the body and focus the mind, imprinting the fundamental techniques on the minds of beginners.

In Kendo today, kirikaeshi is used for the same purpose, although clearly training methods have been modified. There is still ingrained in Kendo a sense that a fidelity to basics leads one to mastery. Then, as now, not all martial artists saw the virtue of such training. Critics of Tesshu's system thought this extreme emphasis on repetition to be foolish and contemptuously termed the training "wood chopping."

Yet Tesshu's purpose was not to create outwardly flashy technique, but to develop the spirit of his trainees. To demonstrate it, he instituted the practice of *seigan* (a Buddhist term meaning "vow"). This training technique was one in which a swordsman first completed one thousand days of successive training, and then was required to stand and continuously face two hundred opponents. If this seigan was successfully completed, the student was eligible, after further training, to undergo a three-day, six-hundred-match seigan. The next and highest level was that of the seven-day, fourteen-hundred-match seigan.

The purpose behind such an intense training method was to consume all of a trainee's physical stamina, to wear down his body and exhaust his technique, until the only thing that drove him to raise his shinai for yet another in a seemingly endless series of matches was the power of the spirit.

We see an echo of Tesshu in modern Kendo's stress on the display of proper spirit in training. We can also acknowledge that the relentless stress on basics in Kendo has been strongly influenced by the ideas of Tesshu and Ittosai.

Given the high value placed on repetition and predictability in training, it is also interesting that both Zen and Kendo place a very strong emphasis on spontaneity, and frequently rely on sudden strong and violent actions to propel the trainee towards enlightenment. In short, both emphasize the importance of experience, and often rely on the unexpected to shock the trainee into awareness.

The unpredictability of Zen masters is legendary: in stories, masters give unexpected, confusing, or illogical answers to sincere and straightforward questions. Sometimes masters don't answer: they strike their disciples or shout at them. These tales are intensely amusing (if you're not the one asking the questions), but what they illustrate is not some cruel streak in Zen training, but rather the conviction that something sudden, unexpected, even painful is sometimes necessary to break the boundaries of normal perception and bring the trainee to a higher plane.

Kendo sensei share both this conviction and this unpredictable, confusing style of behavior. They, too, possess the Zen master's insight into something that defies logical expression or rational thought. They also possess a real knack for confusing their pupils.

In Zen, questions that appear to have no logical answers, termed *koan*, are often used as a vehicle to assist people in making a spiritual breakthrough. The process involves effort, frustration, and confusion, as well as the surprise and terror that the Zen master sometimes creates.

The ultimate experience of confusion for the Kendoka is not koan, but shiai. The experience of engaging in a contest match with your instructor is as dramatic, frightening, and potentially painful as the *mondo* (question and answer session) with the unpredictable Zen master.

Kendo comes alive and has meaning in the experience of practice matches. The opportunity to engage in keiko with one's sensei is an occasion that is both anticipated and dreaded. Here the instructor attempts to elicit the best from the pupil, to push the trainee to the limits of skill and endurance, and sometimes beyond them. Although Kendo is practiced with bamboo staves and protective armor, there is nothing so deadly serious, so intimidating, as engaging in a match with a Kendo sensei. The heated clash and thrust of this combat burns away all illusion and pretense on the trainee's part, and graphically illustrates how well or how poorly the lessons of the art have been learned.

Only in actual practice of Kendo can you come to understand the commonality between the spiritual dimension of Kendo and some of what Zen seeks. Once you raise the shinai in contest, there is no time for thought or reflection. You are immersed in a rapid flow of events, which, like the Zen search for enlightenment, demands a focus on and attention to the here and now that is as exhilarating as it is disconcerting.

Above all, there is a link between Zen and Kendo because both put forth two related and yet seemingly contradictory ideas. One is that the training involved in either discipline is meant to permit the individual to transcend ordinary reality. Thus, for Kendoka, the end point of all this training is to develop a spiritual perspective that is concerned with more than just Kendo. The second idea is that the only way to transcend the discipline you are engaged in is to become immersed in it. Whether it is through the seated meditation practiced by Zen Buddhists or the "moving meditation" of Kendo, only by becoming one with the activity do we have the hope of achieving the integration that both promise.

This was what generations of swordsmen were attempting to hint at in their thoughts on their training. Some articulated it in Zen-like terms, some did not. All, however, seem to hint that there is something more, the "added dimension" mentioned earlier, to the study of martial arts.

To a great extent, the varying philosophical emphases that developed around martial training demonstrated a broad unifying theme that was expressed in differing ways, depending on the predilections of the various masters. All increasingly came to see a strong link between mental, psychological, or spiritual states and physical mastery, and the conviction that some sort of transcendence can be achieved. And this emphasis has endured to the present day.

Ultimately, however, they can only hint at this, since the true experience of this insight comes only through practice that unites mind, spirit, and body into one focused entity.

Which is as good a place to end our discussion as any: to experience even a part of this transcendence, we must practice the art. No amount of thought about Kendo can replace the experience of doing Kendo. It is with time and practice that Kendo's real significance can begin to be appreciated:

That by accepting discipline we are liberated.
In the rush of conflict we find calm.
In the pursuit of self-perfection we are joined with others.
And that only by learning to pick up the sword
Can we develop the wisdom to put it down again.

GLOSSARY

aikido   "way of harmony" a modern budo form that emphasizes spiritual mastery for the development of technical proficiency in its throws, locks, and immobilizations

aizome   special blue dye used in making martial arts uniforms

ashisabaki   footwork

ayumiashi   normal walk, a stride

bakufu   "tent government," term used to describe a military dictatorship in feudal Japan

bogu   Kendo armor

bokken	wooden sword used in martial arts training; also known as a bokuto
budo	martial ways, often used to signify modern martial arts with diminished combat utility and enhanced philosophical components
budoka	martial arts practitioner
bujutsu	martial techniques, a term commonly used in contrast to "budo" and signifying for many a more combat-oriented martial system
bushi	warrior
chi	wisdom
chika-ma	close interval
chu	loyalty
chudan no kamae	middle stance taken in Kendo
daimyo	"great names," the lords of feudal Japan
daisho	two swords (one long, one short), worn by the samurai
dan	category used to describe the rank of advanced practitioners in budo
debana waza	technique of forestalling by attacking at the start of the opponent's action

do	way or path
do	chest protector used in Kendo
dojo	training hall
dojo kun	dojo precepts, often recited at the close of practice sessions
doshu	formal title of the heir to the control of a particular budo form or school
gedan no kamae	low stance
gi	training uniform in arts such as judo and karate consisting of jacket and trousers
gi	honor
go	Japanese board game emphasizing strategy
hachimaki	cloth used as a head covering under the men; also known as a tenegui
hajime	begin
hakama	pleated, divided skirt worn in some budo forms
hanmi	oblique stance commonly used in some forms of swordsmanship and aikido
hanshi	master fencer of eighth through tenth dan
hantei	judgment, decision

hara	lower abdomen, the center of the body, where ki is focused
haragei	form of intuition
harai waza	warding off technique
hashi	boundary line of a match area
hasso no kamae	stance with shinai held at right side of head
haya-suburi	striking practice done while quickly moving toward then away from the target
hidari	left
hikiwake	a draw, in a Kendo match
hiki waza	technique executed by stepping back
himo	strings
hodoku	a special "dead" posture assumed to signal nonaggressive intent
iaido	modern budo form that teaches the art of drawing, cutting with, and sheathing the Japanese long sword through a series of solo exercises
in/yo	Japanese phrase for yin/yang, the active and passive forces in the universe
ippon	one point

issoku-itto no ma	basic distance taken in Kendo, where one step forward will bring the swordsman into striking range
jin	benevolence
jiyu-renshu	free fighting in Kendo
jodan no kamae	stance taken with the sword held high above the head
ju	gentleness, flexibility
judo	"gentle way," a modern budo form based on empty-hand techniques which emphasize throwing, wrestling, and a variety of other techniques
judogi	judo practice uniform
judoka	one who practices judo
jujutsu	techniques of gentleness, the combat-oriented predecessor of judo
jutsu	system of techniques
kaeshi waza	deflecting a shinai by using the reflexive power received by a strike
kai	association, a modern term for martial arts schools
kakari-geiko	attack practice

kake-goe	shout used to demonstrate spirit and focus; typically the word shouted is the intended target area, e.g., "Men!"
kamae	posture, stance; also used as an abbreviated form of gedan no kamae, the most commonly assumed stance in Kendo training
kami	a term used to identify the gods of the Shinto pantheon; its literal meaning is "superior"
kamiza	deity seat, the shrine of the dojo; sometimes referred to as the shomen
kan	hall, a name used to identify a martial arts school
kansetsu waza	joint locks
kappo	resuscitation techniques
karate-do	empty-hand fighting system, which utilizes strikes, kicks, and blocks with the hands, feet, and other parts of the body
kata	stylized sequence of techniques used in martial arts training
katana	Japanese long sword
katsujinken	"the sword that gives life," part of a motto of Yagyu swordsmen
keiko	practice; literally "to reflect on old things"

keikogi	upper part of the practice uniform worn in budo
ken zen ichi mi	"the goals of the sword and that of zen are the same," a Kendo training motto
Kendo	"way of the sword," a modern budo form based on sword techniques of feudal Japan
Kendoka	one who practices Kendo
kenjutsu	sword techniques, Japanese fencing
kenshi	swordsman
keppan	blood oath
ki	universal energy
kiai	shout used in budo training to express and help foster the unity of mind, body, and ki
kihon	basics
kirakaeshi	repetition of Kendo strokes, a formalized exercise in Kendo's basic techniques
kiriotoshi	single technique that formed the basis of the Itto Ryu
kissaki	the point of a sword
koan	seemingly insoluble riddles used in Zen to propel a student into enlightenment
kobujutsu	classical martial techniques

kobun	the status of a child in interpersonal relationships
kodachi	short sword
koh	piety
kohai	juniors, lower-status budoka
kote	protective mitts, which form part of Kendo armor
kuji-in	ritual hand postures used in budo to encourage the development of esoteric powers
kumi-uchi	grappling techniques used by feudal samurai
kumite	sparring
kuzushi	breaking an opponent's balance
kyu	category of beginner's rank in budo training
kyudo	Japanese archery
ma-ai	combative engagement distance
makimono	hand-lettered scrolls that record the secrets of a ryu
mate	wait, pause
mei jin	master
men	head and face covering that makes up a part of the armor in Kendo
men-buton	winglike cotton sides of the men

men-tori	command to remove men at the close of practice
menkyo	a teaching license given to advanced students in traditional martial forms
metsuke	point of observation
michi	way
migi	right
mikkyo	esoteric disciplines
mokuso	meditative sitting
mondo	question and answer session used by Zen masters to lead disciples to enlightenment
montei	disciple
mudra	hand gestures and configurations that in Esoteric Buddhism are thought to facilitate enlightenment
mushin-no-shin	"mind of no-mind," a Zen term
muto	"no-sword," the empty-hand techniques of the Yagyu Ryu as well as the name of Yamaoka Tesshu's school of Itto-ryu swordsmanship
nage waza	throwing techniques of judo and aikido
naginata	a type of pole-arm used by the samurai
nidan waza	two step technique

nuki waza	technique involving a dodge
oji waza	to defend or parry and then immediately counter with a technique
okugi	hidden or esoteric aspects of budo
okuriashi	the sliding step commonly used in Kendo
onegaishimasu	"please practice with me," the phrase used to begin practice with a partner
osae waza	immobilization and pinning techniques
randori	freedom of action, the judo practice of free fighting
rei	bow
reigi	etiquette
renshi	fencer of fourth to sixth dan
renshu	practice period
ri	masterful integration of theory with action
ryu	tradition, the name used to identify a martial arts school
sage-to	position used to carry the sword into the practice or performance area
saika tanden	lower abdomen; alternate for hara
sakigawa	leather tip of shinai

samurai	warrior class of feudal Japan
sandan waza	three-step technique
sankyo	crouching position used in Kendo
satori	Sanskrit term for enlightenment
satsujinken	"the sword that takes life," part of a motto of Yagyu swordsmen
sayu-men	alternate strikes to the left and right sides of the men
seishin	spirit
seishi o choetsu suru	the action of transcending thoughts of life and death
seishin tanren	"spiritual forging," the goal of all budo training
seiza	formal seated position used for meditation and ceremonial activities in budo
sempai	seniors, higher-ranking budoka
sen	initiative
sensei	teacher
shiai	contest
shiaijo	contest area
shidachi	defender in Kendo no kata
shikake waza	an offensive technique of catching an opponent off guard and attacking

shimpan	referee
shin	sincerity
shin-budo	modern budo
shinai	training sword made of bamboo strips used in modern Kendo
shinai-geiko	shinai training, an early term for Kendo training
shinken shobu	literally "real sword contest", a fight to the death
shiromusashi	type of training jacket, frequently worn by young Kendoka in modern times
shizentai	natural stance
shodan	first dan
shogun	military dictator
shomen	another name for the kamiza
shomen-uchi	strike to the head
shoshinsha	beginner in Kendo
sojutsu	spear techniques
suburi	repetitious training of basic strokes in Kendo
suki	gaps in awareness and defense during combat or contest
sumi-e	style of black ink painting

sumo	a form of wrestling
suriage waza	warding off a shinai by sliding your shinai up, permitting you to launch an attack
tachi	long sword
taikai	tournament
taiko	great drum often used to give signals in dojo
tare	hip protector worn in Kendo
tatami	mat
te-hodoki	"untying of hands," a probationary period for students in the classical martial ryu
tenegui	other name for hachimaki
tenouchi	gripping the shinai
to-ma	distant interval
tsuba	hand guard on a sword or shinai
tsuba zerai	Kendo technique of immobilizing an opponent's shinai at the hand guard
tsuka	leather handle cover of a shinai
tsuki	thrust
tsukuri	pulling action used to get an opponent off balance
uchi-dachi	aggressor in Kendo no kata

uchikomi	attack practice
uchima	see issoku-itto no ma
uchiotoshi waza	striking a shinai down and then attacking
uke	partner, the person being thrown
ukemi	breakfall techniques
waza	technique
wakigamae	stance taken holding the sword at the right side, tip pointing to the rear and down
wakizashi	short sword
waza	a technique
wu-hsing	Chinese phrase for five elements, a school of philosophy
yame	finish, a command used in martial arts training
yin/yang	passive and active principles thought to underlie all phenomena
yu	courage
yudansha	dan holder, an individual holding a black belt
zanshin	awareness, in Kendo, the quality of maintaining good form and follow-through after delivering a strike

zarei	formal bow from a seated position
zazen	meditative sitting
Zen	school of Buddhism with a strong influence on martial arts
Zen Nippon Kendo Renmei	All Japan Kendo Federation
zendo	Zen training hall